BEACON HILL

A Walking Tour

Photographs by
William Clift

Drawings by
Robert Polomski

LITTLE, BROWN
AND COMPANY
Boston — Toronto

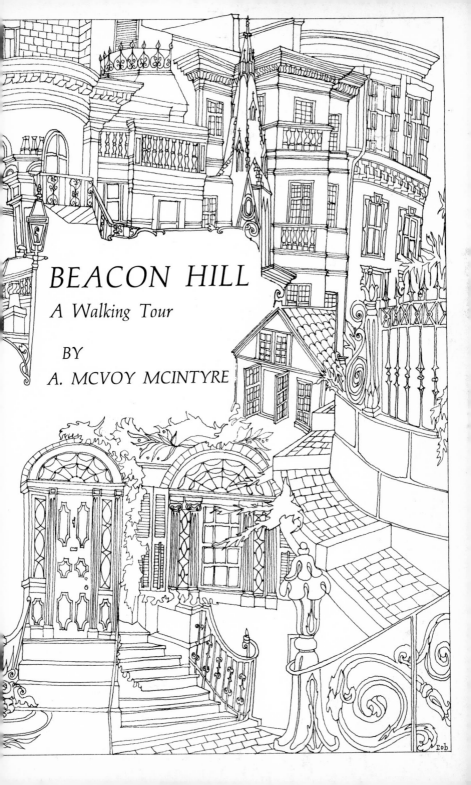

BEACON HILL

A Walking Tour

BY

A. MCVOY MCINTYRE

FIRST EDITION

T 09/75

LIBRARY OF CONGRESS CATALOGING IN PUBLICATION DATA

McIntyre, Alex McVoy.
  Beacon Hill : a walking tour.

    1.   Beacon Hill, Boston.   2.   Boston — Description —
1951-   — Tours.   I.   Title.
F73.68.B4M32   917.44'61   75-16449
ISBN 0-316-55600-9

DESIGN BY BARBARA BELL PITNOF

*Published simultaneously in Canada
by Little, Brown & Company (Canada) Limited*

PRINTED IN THE UNITED STATES OF AMERICA

William Clift dedicates the photographs
in this book to his grandmother, the late
Mrs. Pierce Pearmain, with whom he
spent many years at 85 Pinckney Street.

Acknowledgments

The Beacon Hill Civic Association gratefully acknowledges the many contributions of its Bicentennial Publication Committee, whose talents, time, and shared commitment to the historic significance of our community made the production of this book possible.

BICENTENNIAL PUBLICATION COMMITTEE

Barbara M. Saulnier, Chairperson

Thomas M. Hill
Roy F. Littlehale, Jr.
A. McVoy McIntyre
Ruth C. McKay
Michael H. Rotenberg
Gail Weesner
Sarah L. Whitridge

Contents

Introduction: Before Bulfinch   1

Beacon Street   7
Mt. Vernon Street   27
Chestnut Street   47
West Cedar Street   63
Pinckney Street   75
Louisburg Square   93
North Slope   101

Glossary   113
Appendix: Architects and Housewrights   116

Introduction: Before Bulfinch

Beacon Hill is not old in the sense that Boston is old. We say that the first Bostonian resided here, and with reference to the Reverend William Blaxton, such is fact. A Cambridge University scholar, Blaxton left England before 1630 with a pack of books — which prompted Van Wyck Brooks to make the poignant observance, "There have been books on the slope of Beacon Hill when the wolves still howled on the summit." However, when Blaxton shared his squatter's rights with John Winthrop, the Puritans chose the waterside. There, in 1634, Boston began and over the years spread in semiannual growth about the harbor.

Before 1800 a mere smattering of frame dwellings existed amidst the pastures and brambles of the northwest heights. Remote on the eminence of Trimountain, the great stone house of John Hancock lorded it over the Common. Built in 1737 by Thomas Hancock to be the finest abode in the colony, this prosperous importer's residence was to become the definition of the Boston "mansion house." Here in lonely splendor it reigned until, in the closing decade of the century, the Commonwealth put up a new State House on its eastern flank. Today, the Hancock House is recalled only by a bronze plaque, and the State House is sadly appendaged. Let us attempt, however, to compose the scene at the time of its construction.

It is 1795. The old port town of Boston is

overcrowded with timber buildings — shops, warehouses, taverns, churches, homes the like of Paul Revere's, all clustering in disorder at the Atlantic's edge. Inland, the reaches of the three hills form a woodsy backdrop to the salty, tar-acrid harbor. The view of the fine new State House atop these salubrious heights inspires the more enterprising Bostonian to turn his back on the familiar sight of wharfs, ship masts, and water and to consider a landward venture. Thus motivated, five prominent and foresighted citizens form a syndicate to purchase considerable hillside of their erstwhile fellow townsman, John Singleton Copley (residing in England since 1774 and lionized for his aristocratic portraiture). Setting themselves up as the Mount Vernon Proprietors, apothecary William Scollay, architect Charles Bulfinch, merchant Jonathan Mason, shipowner Joseph Woodward, and lawyer-speculator-politician Harrison Gray Otis begin an association which was to impress indelibly the face of the city.

The Copley purchase extended eighteen and a half acres, roughly along Beacon Street from Charles to Walnut and northward to Pinckney. The price of $18,000 was paid the disgruntled artist. Copley believed that his Boston agent had been outtraded, though he was realizing several hundred percent of an original investment of $3,000. He sent to America his son (later distinguished as England's Lord Chancellor) to repudiate the transaction. The future Lord Lyndhurst's Atlantic voyage was in vain, for he found the deed legally binding, although the Mount Vernon Proprietors from time to time were to defend it zealously due to lack of records verifying the Copley acquisitions.

Forthwith, plans are drawn to level the summits, to impose a grid of streets, to subdivide the land, and to construct dwellings adequate for housing the affluence of the China trade. Thus begins the domestication of Beacon Hill, which in spurts and pauses continues for half a century.

A rambler's first impression is the pleasing homogeneity of the street scene. Observed more closely, the unbroken frontage is a composition of quite individual facades. Within a short block may be seen three distinct styles of house design. Here, as in no other city, the development of this country's urban architecture is documented. There are telltale characteristics. The arched entrance defines the Federal style, an adaptation of the English Georgian which flourished from 1800 to the late 1820's. The post-lintel doorway bespeaks Greek Revival, an American expression from the 1830's to the midcentury. The heavy-scaled, large-proportioned portal describes the Victorian, an eclectic potpourri current from 1850 through the 1890's.

Today, Beacon Hill is a generic locale inclusive of the entire enclave bounded by four streets that parallel the directions of the compass — Beacon on the south, Bowdoin east, Cambridge north and Charles west. The hill's southwest side is Boston's first real estate development. Simultaneously, as so often happens in the probing of new pursuits, the nineteenth century concept of town planning was formulating in parts geographically remote. Thomas Cubitt was guiding the growth of London into Knightsbridge and Belgravia. Robert Adam was laying out New Town for Edinburgh's expansion. So it was with the Mount Vernon Proprietors.

The first buildings were custom designed. No doubt, Harrison Gray Otis gave Bulfinch specific criteria for each of the successive mansion houses planned for his menage. But the fact is that economic realities were soon to determine the shape of things. Buildings in pairs, even blocks, were constructed for speculation. Architects were involved from the beginning, but by far the greater proportion of houses were designed and put up by carpenter craftsmen. These master builders are referred to in ancient deeds as housewrights. To them, mostly unknown and unsung, is due the architectural integrity of Beacon Hill.

Beacon Street

O N THE OLDEST of Beacon Hill streets the walk begins. Gain a vantage on the corner of the Common at the crossing of Beacon and Charles. Look westward. At the beginning of the last century you would have seen water. The tidal estuary known as Back Bay extended southward below the Common to a narrow strip called the Neck, which connected the Boston peninsula with Roxbury.

In 1821 a dam across this backwater, shown on old maps as Roxbury Flats, was constructed to harness the tides for commercial enterprise. Referred to as the Mill Dam, it provided a logical extension to Beacon Street. Upon its eastern abutment in 1828 was erected a block of houses. These six proud edifices, now *Numbers 70 to 75 Beacon Street,* typify the best in local tradition. The kindred faces were given lavish fronts of white Chelmsford granite to attract residents to the new roadway. Harrison Gray Otis built the first two, giving *Number 71* to his son William as a wedding present. The next four were put up by the other Mount Vernon Proprietors.

This is our first encounter with the work of Asher Benjamin. Benjamin was a devotee of Bulfinch and, after Bulfinch, the most sensitive practitioner of the Federal style. He was one of the very few who, with native talent, long apprenticeship, and avid study of English building manuals, was an acknowledged architect.

His national influence on the incipient architectural fraternity was exerted through the publication and republication of his seven copybooks, which spread the Bulfinch-Benjamin interpretation of the Adamesque up and down the Atlantic seaboard. We will meet him again on our walk.

Before turning away, note the distinctive details of *Number 70*. The exterior remains unchanged except for the oriel window, a fanciful but happy addition of a later generation. The scale of the stone coursing, rusticated to the second floor, is comfortably proportioned to the size of the house. The graceful segmental arched treatment forming the entrance and surrounding the tall windows, which are set in a stone transitional panel to accommodate the folded-open blinds, is ingeniously conceived. The touch of ironwork and the guilloche meander of the wooden frieze, repeated on the entrance door, are subtle embellishments.

Proceeding up the street, we will become aware that the higher the ascent, the older the house. This is no quirk of circumstance. The harbor-bound Bostonian was convinced that the summit of the hills possessed the healthy, odor-free atmosphere for a household. Keeping to the sidewalk bordering the Common for the across-street view, note in passing the handsome classic structure on the corner of Charles Street. This is architecture of 1890, the work of the noted New York firm, McKim, Mead and White, and is Beacon Hill's slight brush with eclectic renaissance. From here for half a block the buildings are, at least, second generation. In 1824 the house at *Number 64* Beacon was at the verge of completion when a fire burst out of the carpenter's shop in the rear yard. Before it abated, six houses east of the alley were consumed. The gutted and charred aftermath was brief. Seemingly before the ashes were cold, reconstruction had begun, and phoenixlike, within a year handsome facades identical to the original design rose again to grace the foot of the hill.

The two houses at the beginning of the slope, *Numbers 64 and 63*, are specimens of a transitional style of new classicism that combines the pleasing features of both the late Federal and early Greek Revival periods. Number 64 was originally built in 1821 by Ephraim Marsh, a housewright, who sold it to Elizabeth Boyer Coolidge for $14,400. It is logical to credit Ephraim Marsh with the refined design of Number 63 as well, since he sold the property in 1824 to James Bryant. His sensitive eye must have assembled from Asher Benjamin's manual the balconied piano nobile, the gentle swell of bay, the paneled lintel, the Doric and Ionic porticoes. Today, these premises are the Rectory and the Church House of King's Chapel.

Note the purple glass in Number 63. These panes were part of a large shipment from Hamburg. The defective coloration, not apparent upon installation, appeared after exposure to the sun, which caused a gradual transformation of the manganese oxide component. A tinted glass windowpane is a proud possession. To the historian it is indicative of an installation between 1818 and 1825. A few other lavender windows exist in two houses further up the street and in one house on Chestnut Street.

A step farther brings us to *Number 61*, in recent years the home of Christian Herter, Governor of Massachusetts and President Eisenhower's Secretary of State. This house is Beacon Hill's pride. From curved cheek of stoop to arched dormer of roof, this is architecture of elegance. The sensitive proportions, the elaborate entrance, the profusion of refined detail, the intricately woven ironwork, the delicate colonnade, all culminate in a design of High Regency that recalls the architecture of the

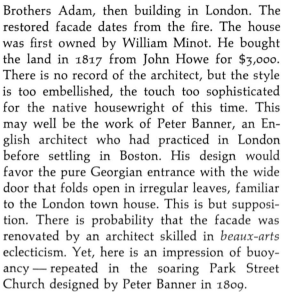

Brothers Adam, then building in London. The restored facade dates from the fire. The house was first owned by William Minot. He bought the land in 1817 from John Howe for $3,000. There is no record of the architect, but the style is too embellished, the touch too sophisticated for the native housewright of this time. This may well be the work of Peter Banner, an English architect who had practiced in London before settling in Boston. His design would favor the pure Georgian entrance with the wide door that folds open in irregular leaves, familiar to the London town house. This is but supposition. There is probability that the facade was renovated by an architect skilled in *beaux-arts* eclecticism. Yet, here is an impression of buoyancy — repeated in the soaring Park Street Church designed by Peter Banner in 1809.

An interesting digression is that Banner collaborated with Solomon Willard on the construction of the Bunker Hill Monument in 1825 — quite a change of pace from Boston's most beautiful attenuated pinnacle to the gravity-conscious monolith of Quincy granite.

The next house, at *Number 60*, with the trim Federal front is the only town house to be yet so used on the rise of Beacon Street. A few doors up, pause at *Numbers 57 and 56*. Built by Ephraim Marsh in 1819, these houses seem to have been designed to respect the architecture of the older pair on the east. These are the original structures. The great fire was stopped at the west wall of Number 57. Marsh sold the plot to David Eckley for $3,250 with a contract to erect a house on it for $13,000. The Eckley contract specified that certain features be similar to those of the house Marsh was currently building at another address — a reference common to the time. "Stone cornice and handsome interior finish" were called for, as was, take note, the advent of the American bathroom: "In the cellar there is to be a bathing room in front into which the aqueduct is to be led." Also provided is a pump in the backyard, "to have a box to hang meat in."

Numbers 55 and 54 were erected in 1807 for James Colburn, a wealthy merchant, and are prototype architecture. They could have materialized directly out of the pages of Benjamin's *Builder's Companion* and are indeed credited to him. Here is a significant Beacon Hill architectural type — the double facade treated in mirror image as a unified composition. Here, too, is first found the bowed bay balanced with the flat frontal entrance, which became a familiar mold for the Greek Revival row house. The definition of the bays with the wooden pilasters is a Bulfinch derivative and may be seen on the front of Number 85 Mt. Vernon Street. An impost member is placed above the column, inserted as a transition between richly carved capital and elaborate cornice in lieu of an architrave. This seems somewhat awkward but a minor flaw. The detailing is Benjamin at his best — light, imaginative, and beautiful.

Number 55 is today owned by the Massachusetts branch of the Colonial Dames of America. As well as a proper present, it has a proper past. Here lived William Hickling Prescott, called the American Thucydides, from 1845 to 1859. Renowned as the authority on Spanish history, Prescott wrote *The Conquest of Mexico,* several fat volumes, from his library desk without ever setting foot in Spain, Mexico, or Peru. This remarkable man, blinded in one eye in an accident at Harvard and rendered nearly sightless by an infection in the other, never able to read for longer intervals than ten minutes, was for years to probe unpublished documents written in Spanish, Italian, and French. He captured world attention in 1837 with the publication of *The Reign of Ferdinand and Isabella,* and for the

first time earned international respect for American scholarship. Spain, debilitated by the Peninsular War, was in too chaotic a state to produce its own historian, and Prescott was recognized as such. Note the commemorative plaque on the left of the door. There is another below in Spanish, presented by the government of Peru.

Number 54 was sold for $13,500 a year after it was built to Nathan Appleton, a prospering young merchant from Ipswich, recently married and establishing himself in Boston. Nathan was proud of his purchase — writing his brother Eben, agent in Liverpool, that the house was all that could be expected "in pleasantness" and "universally allowed to be the cheapest house which had been sold in this town this long time. I could take it to three thousand advance any day." The Nathan Appletons enjoyed the pleasantness of Number 54 until they moved to a house of their own building farther up the hill, where we will again encounter them. Number 54 was sold to cousin William Appleton for $14,000 with an additional $1,000 for "glasses" (two floor-to-ceiling parlor mirrors).

Number 53, a "little birdcage of a house," so called by Fanny Appleton Longfellow, was built in 1855 by another Appleton, "Aunt Sam," widow of Samuel. Cousin William permitted the cornice of the new house to overhang his property. The facade remains little changed. The interior contains a grand circular staircase which, survivor of a fire that wrecked the interior, is now subject of a covenant to remain changeless.

In the next block we pass *Number 48*, a sliver of a building towering awkwardly with the mien of not belonging. Built about 1900, its twelve stories aroused Boston to enact legislation restricting building heights: the first of its kind in America.

The double brownstone facade with Back Bay pretensions at *Number 46* is the renovation of two houses for the latter-day Boston merchant prince, Eben Jordan. The interior is palatial with every sort and condition of eclectic grandeur.

We are now at a notable address, *Number 45.* An "elegant new house" was the aesthetic assessment recorded by the town assessors in 1806 on completion of this stone and brick mansion house, which vied with the Hancock estate for command of Beacon Street. Elegance characterized not only the house, but both its owner and architect. In Federal Boston, Harrison Gray Otis was acknowledged arbiter of the social scene and Charles Bulfinch its Christopher Wren. Such a happy relationship proved a lasting boon to this city. All three mansion houses that Otis commissioned of Bulfinch still grace Beacon Hill. We know them numerically. The first was built in 1796 on Cambridge Street. The second, built in 1802, we will see on Mt. Vernon Street.

This is the third — now headquarters for the American Meteorological Society. It was Otis's home for forty-two years and the house associated with the lore accumulated over the years from the momentum of a vigorous life. Originally the structure stood free, with its east side gracefully bowed to form the oval room so admired of the period. This gave onto a spacious garden which, graded into the slope of the hill, was a level above the street entrance. The prominent feature of the front facade is the piano nobile, expressed here with flawless grace. The deep windows, defined in a classic wood framing with bracketed lintel, once commanded a splendid view over the green pasture of the Common and across the waters of Back Bay to the Blue Hills. The central window is accented with the relief of an eagle proclaiming the new republic. Windows of lesser height repeat the sequence in the upper floors. A carved keystone is their only accent. The rich entablature is typically of wood — such fine detail in stone was unobtainable at this period. The roofline is emphasized with a hand-turned balustrade which, as the final and unifying element, completes the aesthetic composition of this subtle yet strong facade.

On the west of the house is a cobbled driveway, off which is the carriage entrance. A short flight of granite steps with a simple iron railing rises to the slight landing that is just short of the width of the doorway. The structure thus avoids an ancient tree growing within a few feet of the house. The doorway motif, slender single columns supporting a classic entablature, is of the same delicacy and detail as the entrances to the three Bulfinch houses on Chestnut Street, Numbers 13, 15 and 17. This recurrence of motif is a kindred tie that gives Beacon Hill architecture its congeniality. Note the intriguing geometry of the railing at balcony and portico, an interplay of the Greek key with the Chinese fret. It is a detail picked up on every other street.

Beyond the side entrance the drive opens into a generous court in front of a large carriage house and stable. The structure offers a pleasing contrast with the residence in the informal treatment of its graceful arched openings. The stable still contains the stalls — but no horses.

Many are the tales of Mr. Otis and his mansion house. The scope of life that filled the beautiful spacious interiors became a legend. The family and its kith and kin were many, congenial, and notoriously well fed. Well known was the blue and white Lowestoft punch bowl on the stair landing as oasis for thirsty guests. Presidents were entertained. Monroe was offered the entire premises. Henry Clay and other notables visiting Boston were welcome at the Beacon Street portal. The mansion in 1828 was the scene of the owner's inauguration as Boston's third mayor. The reception for municipal rank and file who roamed through the lavish interiors was unprecedented.

At the time of the great fire a fierce north-wester was showering burning fragments with the force of a hailstorm. Mr. Otis had the good judgment to cover his roof with wet blankets, which saved the house. The only fire loss that could be claimed was that of his cellar. Beacon Street was chockablock with Sheraton and Chippendale furniture and Aubusson carpets as furnishings were moved out of the threatened houses. Bottles of Madeira which had not seen the light of day for twenty years proved too tempting to the parched firemen, and when the spectators proceeded to join in, the firelit scene took on aspects of a Neroesque bacchanalia.

By 1831, when Mr. Otis was approaching seventy, his hereditary Yankee shrewdness overcame the cavalier ways of earlier years. Perhaps well-earned gout limited perambulation about the fine east garden. There it was, fifty feet of virgin Beacon Hill frontage at a time when such land had never been more valuable. In 1831 Mr. Otis and neighbor Colonel David Sears could resist no longer a real estate orgy and fell to with a vengeance. Colonel Sears bought the eastern-most half of the garden for $12,412.50, and the remaining twenty-five feet was prepared by Otis for building. Within a year the new houses of these gentlemen were abutting. The Sears premises at *Number 43* took on a second round bay. Mr. Otis's new building at *Number 44* carried over the theme, if not the finesse, of the Bulfinch original. The party wall bows with the bay of the older house, creating a concave interior unique to the hill. Upon the completion of this house, Mr. Otis arranged with legal rectitude that his daughter and "affection," Sophia Ritchie, possess this property.

In reading the deed of sale one notes the precision with which Otis and Sears, neighbors for more than a decade and warm friends, handled such transactions. Very carefully the deed stipulates the observance of setback, allowing no other structure "except dwelling houses with a swelled front, the swell of which only, if such there be, may project as far southerly and no further than the swell on the front of said Sears present mansion house."

And next at *Number 42* is the Sears mansion house with its two front swells. The building, designed by Alexander Parris (his first Boston commission), was a two-storied structure with a single domed central bay in admiration of the Mount Vernon estate of Sears's father-in-law, Jonathan Mason. Built by 1819, this weighty edifice introduced Greek Revival architecture in Rockport granite to the local scene. Evidently pleased with his efforts, Parris had his name cut in the stone of the basement wall. The fine rectilinear cartouches were carved by the architect's peer, Solomon Willard, who was also engineer, stonemason, botanist. In 1872, one hundred and two years after John Singleton Copley departed this site for England, the Somerset Club acquired the property. A third floor has since been added, the flat east bay given a street entrance, and the entire frontage well bastioned by a rusticated wall which is pierced by an iron-studded portal serving, somewhat overstatedly, as the kitchen entry. This is Beacon Hill's only baronial touch.

At *Number 39* we again find Nathan Appleton, who by 1820 built this mansion, persuading his former mercantile partner, Daniel Pinckney Parker, to put up its twin. Appleton had become progenitor of the New England textile manufacturer. On the architectural scene, it is believed that Alexander Parris, with the Sears house to his credit, here furthered his professional career. The design, in its grasp of large scale and use of stone detail, recalls a bold classic treatment — "Greek Revival in gestation," writes Talbot Hamlin, the dean of architectural historians. The fourth floor was added with ad-

mirable sense of proportion and style by Hart-
well and Richardson in 1888. At the same time
a middle window joined the original two in the
bow of Number 39.

From the exterior, this second-floor fenestration identifies the parlor where Fanny Appleton
married Henry Wadsworth Longfellow in 1843.
In the same decade this beautiful mansion received, less cordially, another literary personage,
Boston-born but not -bred Edgar Allan Poe. At-
tending an Appleton soiree, Poe evidently be-
haved in a way his host considered improper,
particularly with ladies present, and was escorted
to the door. In next morning's letter of apology
the poet denied inebriation, claiming that merely
having a good time in pleasant company affected
him as wine might affect other people! Boston,
so tolerant of idiosyncrasy and abounding with
personal oddity, yet looked askance upon genius.
Unhappy, sensitive poet, reacting to the all too
general uncompromising disapproval, Poe was
wont to refer to his native city as "Frogpondium."

Today, the twin facades, joined together as
the Women's City Club, seem to beam with
hospitality.

Observe, as we cross Walnut Street, the
square mansard-roofed structure on the corner.
Its Victorian classicism is the result of multi-
facelifting. Originally, Beacon Street's first brick
house (the Hancock house was of stone), it was
built in 1804 by John Phillips, Boston's first
mayor and the father of Wendell. An old water-
color shows a proper Federal facade — central
entrance on Beacon Street approached from a
flight of steps. The roof is of a low-pitched,
hipped construction. In a later sketch the mansard and lintel shelf are added, and the entrance,
a simple off-centered arch, has moved to Walnut
Street. Today, only the small salmon-colored
bricks recall its original construction.

At the upper end of the short block, *Number 34½*, at the corner of Joy, is the endlessly fascinating composition of angularly stepped facades embellished with bay windows, gables, and statuesque chimneys, all wrought of stone and brick. Representative of the Kenilworth school of late Victorian architecture, it replaced older houses at this prominent location. It is called Tudor after an owner of an earlier house on this site, Frederick Tudor, who had the ingenuity to sell Charles River ice, harvested by the shipload with a cutting machine of his own invention, to natives of the West Indies.

Across Joy the two brick and stone mansions on the corner, *Numbers 34 and 33*, are a handsome variation of architectural style. They were built in 1825 by architect-housewright Cornelius Coolidge and are another expression of the transition from Federal to Greek Revival. Note the similarity of entrance treatment with Alexander Parris's houses at Numbers 39 and 40.

The house on the right has been home to dramatis personae of fact and fiction. Those familiar with the bestseller list of the 1930's may recall reading George Santayana's *Last Puritan*. In a Beacon Hill setting of the 1870's when, on every Tuesday and Friday at half-past eleven, Mr. Nathaniel Alden stepped from his front door onto Beacon Street, always turning to the left, "for never, except to funerals, did Mr. Nathaniel Alden walk down Beacon Hill," he exited from Number 33. From more poignant references to Mr. Alden's past it becomes evident to a literary sleuth that Santayana had in mind George Francis Parkman. Here fact takes over.

In the 1850's Beacon Hill captured international notoriety with a murder trial dramatized in a production that could have upstaged Barnum. Its most respected jurist, Judge Lemuel Shaw, presided. The defendant, John White Webster, was a Harvard professor. Character witnesses were such worthies as Dr. Oliver Wendell Holmes and Harvard President Jared Sparks ("our professors do not often commit murder"). And the victim, the most socially distinguished in the annals of American crime, was Dr. George Parkman, father of George Francis. This episode is vividly described in Cleveland Amory's *Proper Bostonians*.

Professor Webster's conviction, with concurrent notoriety, left the bereaved Parkmans little choice but to retire from the curious gaze in dignified, first-family seclusion. In 1853 George Francis Parkman, with his mother and sister, took possession of Number 33 Beacon Street. For over half a century this gracious facade screened the mundane activities of Beacon Hill from the sensitive recluses. The death of his mother brought no visible change to Mr. Parkman's social routine. Biweekly excursions to the

Athenaeum provided sufficient contact with worldly Boston for a patterned life consisting, according to local gossip, of observing through closed blinds of second-story windows the antics of squirrel and pigeon on the Common below. In 1908 he died, and the city found itself heir to the beautiful old mansion and a bequest of six million dollars.

A news item at this time in the Boston *Evening Transcript* implies that for all their seclusion, the Parkmans lived up to their means. On January 11 and 12 in 1909, an auction was held at Number 33 Beacon to dispose of the household effects. The gray, wet Monday, so typical of a Boston January, did not dampen the ardor of prospective buyer, neighbor and acquaintance. The newspaper reports crowded rooms and "spirited bidding." The auction was most successful, the article concludes, suggesting that New York relatives kept the going price at high levels. A Duncan Phyfe sofa brought $600; chairs of "antique design" from $15 to $30; a pair of ornate brass mantle lamps with crystal pendants, $177.50. One hundred and twenty pieces of Nanking and Canton china went for $100. On the second day the rumored activities and the opportunity to get through unfrequented portals attracted all that the spacious rooms could hold. A Paul Revere silver ladle was the most bid-for item, bringing $400. Boston chauvinism as an economic factor was quite evident when comparable George III pieces were knocked down at $6. Of the general excitement aroused, a renowned wit was overheard to comment, "And why not? A Parkman dies just once in a lifetime." Today, this legended landmark has been refitted to offer the hospitality of the city as its Guest House.

As we gain the eminence of the hill and before we are captivated by the presence of the capitol, observe on the Park Street corner that

assemblage of all manner of aggressive ex-
crescence. This is the very model, in a socio-
logical perspective, of what the indiscriminate
unconcern of generations hath wrought upon an
old, historic building.

Here was once a beautiful and proud residence, in command of its imposing site. A square
brick building as Bulfinch conceived it — there
were formal entrances from both Beacon and
Park Streets to what must have been at least
two households.

The view of the Common doubtless decided
the architectural orientation, for the Park Street
frontage was treated with much richness. Old
photographs show an elaborate panoply of ellip-
tical stairs, delicate iron balconies, graceful
portico, deep architraved windows, balustered
parapet — all proportioned with the consummate skill of the architect. Today, alas, only the
wide arched transom, a curve of steps, and four
paint-encrusted Corinthian columns suggest such
a picture.

Thomas Amory built the house in 1804 but
lost his fortune before establishing residence. It
became the first of Boston's apartments for housing the elite. Samuel Dexter, cabinet officer
under President Adams, and Fisher Ames, member of Congress, were tenants. Christopher Gore,
while Massachusetts governor, commuted from
his Waltham estate to this, his Boston residence.
In 1824 the city leased these appropriate accom-
modations for General Lafayette when he was
guest at the dedication of the Bunker Hill Monument. In 1830 the great house was to have a
renaissance when acquired by George Ticknor
for his home. Professor Ticknor, of Harvard's
Department of Romance Languages, occupied
possibly only the Park Street portion, but all of
Beacon Hill was identified with his scholarly
renown. Shelved here was the best library of
midcentury America — thousands of books des-

tined to become the nucleus of the Boston Public Library. The interior is visualized by Van Wyck Brooks: ". . . housed in the largest and most elegant room, approached through a marble hall by a marble stairway, about which the butler discreetly hovered." George Ticknor was early of that breed, the Boston Brahmin; intelligent, guileless, superbly educated, conscience-driven, wealthily bred and wed, but above all, possessed with a sense of noblesse oblige.

It was by and for patrons like George Ticknor that the Boston Athenaeum was established — and flourishes. If ever one institution can be all things to all men this private library so serves the Boston book-lover. At *Number 10½*, just before Beacon turns sharply southward and pitches downhill to become School Street, is the Athenaeum's rather formidably dark and classically proper frontage.

Incorporated in 1807, it had outgrown by 1847 a series of converted residences and moved to an imposing structure designed for it on Beacon Street by Edward C. Cabot. The facade (of Paterson freestone, a hard and dense limestone) is that we see today, weathered and sooted to a time-honored patina. From across the street is visible a higher and newer setback that completely envelops all but the front wall of the older structure, more than doubling its original size. This expansion was necessary in the years 1913–1914 and accomplished with consummate skill and taste by the architect, Henry Forbes Bigelow. The interior, according to David McCord, "combines the best elements of the Bodleian, Monticello, the frigate *Constitution*, a greenhouse, and an old New England sitting room."

This institution has endeared itself to generations of Bostonians who have bequeathed it their substance, their furniture, and their art, making it a repository of culture as well as of scholarship. Beacon Hill has always been well represented here. Harrison Gray Otis was an original trustee; Alexander Parris was the forty-seventh proprietor; Solomon Willard was a donor and life subscriber.

Returning to the State House, we find an American heritage. Red brick and white colonnaded, the midcentral element of the bewinged complex atop the hill is Beacon Hill's oldest and noblest architecture. Charles Bulfinch is Boston's first architect. During the opening era of the republic he created out of the English Georgian a style which is distinctly indigenous, American Federal.

The history of the capitol begins with the dramatic choice of site — just short of Beacon Hill's original summit. For architect it was logical to look to young Bulfinch, a fourth-generation Bostonian, Harvard-trained, European-traveled, who had eschewed the countinghouse of his merchant kinsmen for the pursuit of "giving gratuitous advice in architecture." After financing a disastrous real estate venture known as the Tontine Crescent, "gratuitous" was dropped and, as was plainly put by Mrs. Bulfinch, "My husband has made architecture his business, as it had been his pleasure." In 1795 he was thirty-two, a selectman, and the committee's choice to design the new State House. On July 4 of that year the cornerstone, drawn up the hill by fifteen white horses (one for every state), was patriotically laid by Governor Samuel Adams and Paul Revere.

The ubiquitous Paul Revere was also to furnish the copper cladding for the dome. Atop was placed the tiaralike lantern with its multipaned windows sparkling in the sun. On its pinnacle was set the gilded carving of a pine cone, emblematic, as noted in an eighteenth century description, "of one of our principal staples."

A day could well be spent inside the capitol building with the guidebook of Sinclair H. Hitchings and Catherine H. Farlow, examining the rooms of state. This book accounts for the various additions, accumulated over the years, which have increased the original size of the State House more than tenfold. Long obscured is the north facade, originally an architectural repetition of the Beacon Street front.

The grounds have also undergone successive expansion, terracing, and embellishment complementary to the architecture. The landscaping project of 1826 added at street level the fine portal with the unique treatment of Greek-fretted ironwork arching between granite piers to grasp the lantern as keystone. Such an inviting feature is the design of Alexander Parris. Colleague Solomon Willard collaborated in the layout of stone retaining walls and the design of iron fencing, now removed. This garnishing of their patron architect's masterpiece is done with an appreciation of grandeur, a sure sense of scale, and, indeed, much respect. The admirer of Federal architecture may linger or return. We must push on into the nineteenth century. Mount the State House steps and pass through the Doric Hall to exit into Mt. Vernon Street as it passes through the building.

Mt. Vernon Street

OF THE GRID of streets that partition Beacon Hill into a pattern as straight and rigid as if laid out by a Puritanical theologian, one must agree with Henry James that Mt. Vernon Street is the most proper. Beacon Street is grand; Chestnut beautiful; Pinckney characterful; West Cedar intimate; but Mt. Vernon expresses that "long view" which a Bostonian likes to take as well as to see.

We are paused at the State House entrance under the bridge of the Brigham addition. Before venturing into Mt. Vernon's spacious scene, we must satisfy a historical conscience. Turn east. Our objective is to locate the original crest of Beacon Hill, which in its colonial eminence bore the beacon decreed by the General Court in 1634, "to give notice of any danger." The beacon stood for years, an uncomely thing consisting of a tall wooden mast at the top of which projected a bracket holding a pot of pitch. The casualty of a storm in 1789, the beacon was considered to have fulfilled its function, and in its stead, a memorial was proposed by Charles Bulfinch, young and eager, who organized a public subscription on its behalf. His early commission from the Commonwealth materialized as a Doric column of plastered brick set on a stone pedestal and attaining a height of sixty feet.

About the base were plaques of slate and, surmounting the shaft, a gilded, heraldic eagle. The original design had envisioned the eagle as a weather vane with the added function of a lightning rod. Erected, the monument was destined for a brief commemoration. In the practical 1800's real estate was dearer than prestige. The hill's exposed flanks and spurs flaunted irresistible sources. So tempted, the city in 1811 sold its birthright, Beacon Hill's summit of "six rods square," complete with monument, for $9,000. It was promptly decapitated, as had been Mount Vernon's summit a decade earlier. At the end of the century, in 1898, civic conscience, long remorseful over the ill-advised destruction, was mollified at the replacement of Bulfinch's column on hallowed if shifted sod. Today, sixty feet below its first elevation and some hundred feet eastward, the single granite shaft, adorned with original eagle and plaques, rises oddly in the midst of crowded cars. It may be hoped that this historic place be restored to the pleasant park it once was.

Retracing steps, turn west on Mt. Vernon Street. The houses on the south corner of Joy command this intersection with indigenous authority. The corner mansion was designed by Alexander Parris in 1824 for George William Lyman, who later acquired its neighbor, *Number 18*. For generations the properties were a family compound. The twain, now handsome town house apartments, are yet interconnected. The Mt. Vernon side, with glimpse of winding stair through arched window, recalls the Federal style. The formal entrance facade fronting Joy is heavily-scaled Greek Revival, interesting for its asymmetry.

We cross Joy Street, which until 1851 was named Belknap. On the southwestern corner of Mt. Vernon Street, first called Olive Street, stood the prototype of the Federal mansion house. In 1805 Bulfinch designed for Thomas Perkins an imposing, squarish, five-story edifice replete with the architect's favorite embellish-

ment — a Regency portico, windows in recessed
arches, inset marble panels, fan-transomed windows with double keystone lintels, and stone
banding. Mr. Perkins, a fastidious Bostonian,
commissioned his agent in London as well as
the American consul in Leghorn, his brother-in-
law, to garner interior embellishments such as
crystal chandeliers and marble mantelpieces.
Bulfinch placed the reception rooms across the
rear with a splendid vista of the Common, and
Mr. Perkins perpetuated the view by a setback
restriction to his Joy Street terraces. After Mr.
Perkins died the beautiful mansion was torn
down and replaced with nondescript Victorian.

On the opposite corner the four original
houses at *Numbers 43, 45, 47 and 49,* were built
in 1803 by Stephen Higginson, Jr. Number 49
survives in part. Conforming to an early concept
of Bulfinch, who may have designed it, the building was planned with a narrow street facade, the
entrance gained from a garden on the west side.
Massachusetts Chief Justice Lemuel Shaw purchased the premises in 1831 and expanded the
house to fill the garden and abut the neighboring
wall. The baroque entrance of brownstone (not
Bulfinch) is indeed a portal to be reckoned with.

The next four houses were built by Jonathan
Mason. Here was a Bostonian to cast the proper
image: son of a deacon, class of Princeton 1774,
well married, father of seven, prominent lawyer,
substantial property owner, United States senator, and patriarchal benefactor. Jonathan Mason
and Harrison Gray Otis were prime movers of
the Mount Vernon Proprietors, responsible for
the basic warp and woof of Beacon Hill.

In 1802 these close friends, hoping to attract
other residents to the sunny slopes, erected great
mansion houses on the broad hillside. Mason's
house, with spacious gardens, occupied land at
the head of Walnut Street, where now half a
block of row houses stand. Bulfinch, a Mount

Vernon Proprietor at this time, designed the
building to a square plan featuring a central bow
at front with entrance vestibule projecting on
the east side. A drawing depicts a three-story
brick edifice set well back from the street and
approached from a circular drive. The floor plan
included a two-storied ballroom behind the cen-
ter bow, allegedly for marrying off five daughters. That the ballroom served its purpose is
evidenced by the Bulfinch-designed daughter
houses built in 1804 at *Numbers 51, 53, 55 and
57*. Number 55 remains unaltered. The distinc-

tive characteristics are all here: arched recesses,
stone banding (note the street name incised at
the corner), and keystone lintels. The molded
brick of the cornice, a standard masonry item
even at this time, is repeated in the wooden trim
of the vestibule. Long the home of a philanthro-

pic Beacon Hill lady, Rose Nichols, the house preserves its donor's hospitality as a neighborly place where friends meet, as well as a historic house-museum.

Number 57 looks over the beautiful garden of the Rose Nichols House and shares details at cornice and window. Bulfinch planned this building to be entered on the west side facing Mr. Mason's circular driveway. The width of street frontage provided for two windows. The house belonged to Mrs. Samuel Parkman, a Mason daughter, who sold it at the division of the Mason estate in 1838 to Cornelius Coolidge. Coolidge extended the house eight feet westward and designed the delightful new entrance in a bold but elegant Greek Revival motif imaginative for this rigid style.

Number 57 Mt. Vernon is a historical address. Daniel Webster was a tenant of Mr. Mason from 1817 to 1819. Later the house was acquired by Webster's political opponent, Charles Francis Adams, minister to England during the Civil War. Adams lived here for over forty years, and his sons, Charles Francis II and Henry, spent their boyhood on Mt. Vernon Street and at Quincy. Charles heartily disliked Mt. Vernon, preferring the old farm, but Henry, allowed a desk in his father's library, the only bright room, was less critical.

Crossing to the south side of the street return to the house at *Number 26*, which is of 1838 vintage, built by Mr. Perkins for his daughter. At one time it was the home of Governor Curtis Guild.

The next four houses, *Numbers 28 to 34*, two windows wide and four stories high, date from 1822 and recognize the trend toward the smaller town house. The triple window at street floor level, typical of Beacon Hill, is introduced at this time as an efficient way to realize optimum light in a narrow room. This block of houses, too, can boast of notables. Number 32 was one of the many Boston homes of Dr. Samuel Gridley Howe, founder of the Perkins Institute for the Blind. His wife, Julia Ward Howe, was an early women's rights enthusiast; she composed and sang upon request "The Battle Hymn of the Republic." The Howes were nationally hospitable. The gamut of their social calendar ranged from reception for President Grant to breakfast for Bret Harte.

The neighboring house with entrance on Walnut Street is early accounted in Beacon Hill lore as "a small house finished for little money, $5,000–$7,000." It was built by John Callender in 1803, becoming the third mansion house on Mt. Vernon Street. The land was bought from Dr. Joy for $2,155. Today, it is whispered, a valuation would be far in excess of $200,000.

Built without benefit of Bulfinch, this great house may be described as refreshingly understated. It is a most interesting survival of that outmoded wall construction of sheathing over brick masonry with tightly joined boards. Even the gray paint is common to the era. At the time of completion the building was entered from Mt. Vernon Street. In 1821 the city reduced the grade of Walnut Street, exposing the foundation and necessitating a granite wall to retain the garden. The entrance was changed to its present location at this time. Mr. Callender unsuccessfully brought suit against the city for damages. In 1835 the house was the rectory for Trinity Church. The Reverend Jonathan Mayhew Wainwright lived here before becoming Bishop of New York.

Before proceeding downhill, cross again to the north side and retrack to *Number 59.* Here is a most admired example of Beacon Hill's reserved acceptance of the flourishing Greek Revival architecture. Erected in 1837 at the time of partitioning the Mason property, the building rec-

ognized the Otis-Mason gentlemen's agreement of thirty-foot setback, setting the pattern for the remainder of the block. Adam Wallace Thaxter, the mathematical instrument maker, built it from plans by Edward Shaw. This is Edward Shaw's only Boston evidence of professional talent and builder's skill. Like Asher Benjamin, Shaw was known far afield for his architectural primers, *Civil Architecture* and *Rural Architecture*. In this house alone can be found inspiration enough for a volume on Greek Revival. The portal is beautifully proportioned and classically chaste. The pedimental lintels, the stone insets with frieze of laurel wreaths, the grilled iron balconies compose an elaborate but refined facade. The cost of the building was $17,000. By the end of the last century it was the home of *Atlantic Monthly* editor Thomas Bailey Aldrich. The family is yet in residence.

The adjoining houses, *Numbers 61, 63, and 65,* cover the actual site of the former Mason mansion. They were constructed in 1837 with the fashionable bow front and proliferation of heavy Victorian brownstone. The large window-panes suggest the glass manufacturer's progress. Number 65, since replaced, was the home of Senator Henry Cabot Lodge.

The rest of this block, all built by 1836, varies little within the heavy Victorian style. *Numbers 71 and 73* recall a Federal treatment at entrance, graceful but somewhat out of scale with the massive facade. *Number 79* housed Horace Gray, for twenty years justice of the Supreme Court, and at *Number 83* resided William Ellery Channing, who may be found in a bronze likeness within preaching distance of his church at Arlington and Boylston streets.

We now come to Mr. Otis's Mt. Vernon estate, the second of his architectural trio. It was constructed in the same year, 1802, to the same grand scale, by the same architect who had

designed the mansion house of fellow Proprietor Jonathan Mason. Otis, a Renaissance character, had instinctive taste and recognition of quality, especially of Charles Bulfinch. The spacious, well-kept setting, the extravagant detail express an expansive life-style that subsequent owners have maintained. The fastidious, closely observing the front facade, may question that the applied treatment of wooden pilaster and entablature does not continue across the entire width of the wall, giving a sense of repose to the design. And the answer may be that Mr. Otis was one for an expansive and fanciful front.

Though much of the original fabric is complete, one hundred and seventy years have seen changes. In the 1850's the original entrance on the east side was removed from mid-wall. A new entrance extension was added to the rear corner and adorned with the full-blown Greek Revival portico. At that time the property was owned by the Misses Pratt, three sisters who had left a fond family home on the corner of Summer and Hawley Streets because of the deterioration of that once residentially fashionable section. When their old home was replaced by a commercial building the sisters, with, it is said, both family sentiment and Boston thrift, had the familiar granite porch and a new rear entrance hall grafted to the Bulfinch facade. Another change occurred in 1882 when the property had passed to the Philip Sears family. The large bow on the west was extended to contain a dining room. This variation of Queen Anne Revival is attributed to the architects, Peabody and Stearns, who are responsible for much of Back Bay. The present century's adaptation is the conversion in recent years of the rear carriage-house ell into a commodious living complex approached off the cobbled courtyard.

The neighbor at *Number 87* is of architectural kin. Bulfinch built the house for his own

occupancy in 1805 with a double to the west, but before completion financial reverses forced him to sell it. The familiar features are here composed in a well-proportioned, ordered design — refined but without the grandeur of the second and third Otis houses or the quiet dignity of the first.

The replacement of the original *Number 89* is fine twentieth century Georgian and quite compatible with its one-time twin.

Turning again to the south side of the street, backtrack to the corner of Walnut Street. The two brownstone houses, *Numbers 40 and 42*, were built in 1850 on the site of a large 1822 mansion. This architectural change of pace is the work of George Dexter. The graceful iron balcony is of components similar to those used by Cornelius Coolidge over the entrance to Number 57, which we have just seen.

Neighbors, *Numbers 44, 46 and 48*, are appealing examples of the small unpretentious house which is found on Chestnut and West Cedar of the decade 1820–1830. The structure is three-storied with dormered roof. The entrances, fan-transomed and sidelighted, are deeply recessed in the arched openings. The individual design of leaded glass and door detail gives intimacy to the common frontage.

The abutting houses, thirteen feet high, add variety to the grandeur of the street. They are renovated stables originally built for the Chestnut Street houses, and contain a lower floor at the rear. The height is a deed restriction imposed by the builder, Mrs. Hepzibah Swan, who was the only female partner of the Mount Vernon Proprietorship. Also imposed is the restriction of maintaining an inclined passage from the street to the lower level, which accounts for the arched double doorway between *Numbers 50 and 56*.

In the 1920's Number 50 was renovated for occupancy by the Club of Odd Volumes. During the transition period from stable to residence this low block was used as artists' studios. The brothers Maurice and Charles Prendergast painted here.

Downhill, the houses at *Numbers 62 and 64* were constructed in 1809 and 1810 for John Trecothick Apthorp, president of the Boston Bank. Adjoining and built in the same year are *Numbers 66 and 68* by Jeremiah Gardner, housewright.

The double granite edifice at *Numbers 70 and 72* confronts us with an abrupt change of era. This considerable structure was put up in 1847 to the design of Richard Upjohn, who had come from England some ten years previously. Mr. Upjohn also designed the fencing for the Common and was the architect for several New York churches. When given up as households, these premises had a varied scholastic career, serving first as a theological seminary, then as an apothecary college. Recently, the commodious building has been made into spacious condominiums, but only after a raging battle had split the community over the attempt at replacement with an apartment complex of twentieth century Georgian design.

Further downhill, *Number 74* was built in 1810 for fashionable upholsterer Moses Grant, to the design of his son-in-law, Cornelius Coolidge. *Numbers 76 and 78* came in 1811 for speculation. Eleven years later *Numbers 82 and 84* were completed, the last of the original houses left on the block. In passing, note the quaint bit of cityscape on the curb of Number 82, an old lamplighter's lamp.

Pause here on the cobbles below the statue of Aristides and due west observe the Meeting House filling the perspective. Its cupola composes a cluster of steeples with the Church of the Advent's flèche and spire. Now, directing our gaze with Aristides, we are looking at two fine facades noteworthy as the prevailing archi-

tecture of Beacon Hill. Side by side, *Numbers 90 and 92*, built but seven years apart, represent the transition from the Federal to the Greek Revival period.

The three-story, single-dormered house with its entrance arched and deeply inset is fine understated Georgian. In the generously proportioned simple facade the doorway sparkles like an ornament. The fan of serpentine tracery and the complementary sidelights set off by a sharply articulated egg and dart molding surround the six-paneled door in Adamesque refinement. The whole composes a graciously inviting portal.

Abutting downhill, *Number 92* is an equally fine expression of Beacon Hill's tempered Greek Revival. The front is bold and features the tall architraved windows of the piano nobile behind a continuous iron balcony. This unpretentious entrance is post-lintel, heavily framed in sandstone. The rectangular transom and sidelights emphasize the simple, austere dignity of this style.

These two houses with their neighbors in the short block from Willow to West Cedar Street are built on the original holding of the Mount Vernon Proprietors. In 1823 the Proprietorship distributed this parcel to individual ownership. Harrison Gray Otis possessed one hundred and thirty-four feet of Mt. Vernon west of Willow Street, Jonathan Mason the remainder to West Cedar. A rather nebulous condition to the division restricted to rising no higher than the parlor floor of the house a "back building" to be built on the adjacent property.

To stimulate the sluggish real estate economy of the 1820's, Otis proceeded with characteristic zest to put up on the corner property two fine mansion houses for lease until sale was profitable. The admired Federal house at *Number 90* remains the oldest on this block. It was built in 1826 with a twin on the east where the apartment building now rises.

The 1830's found Boston's merchants again prospering. The old town of two centuries, now a city, felt an odd pulsation of expansiveness. The population had reached 61,392. New building was everywhere. With patriotic fanfare, Asher Benjamin, the era's Bulfinch, introduced the "Grecian Style" to the Boston housewright in his 1833 builder's manual, *Practice of Architecture*. "Its economical plan and plain massive features are peculiarly adapted to the Republican habits of this country."

On Beacon Hill construction activity focusing in Louisburg Square spilled down Mt. Vernon. The Otis land at *Number 92* was sold in 1833 for $3,160 to George B. Stearns, who by the next year had built his house in the new Grecian style. Records show that Mr. Stearns, who had spent over $12,000 in the building, had overextended, and the proud edifice a few years after completion began its Mt. Vernon tenure with a sheriff's sale.

The next house, at *Number 94*, a "messuage" built by William Frost in 1835, was sold for $13,000 to Matthew Bolles. Good neighbor Bolles permitted Jesse Shaw, housewright, and Alanson Rice, mason, for the consideration of $1 to erect on an adjacent site a back building higher than his parlor windows. This is *Number 96*. The lot, the last of Otis's Mt. Vernon holding, was bought in 1833 at a cost of $2,730 and sold in 1835 with the "brick mansion house" to Samuel Frothingham for $14,500. It may be that Shaw and Rice constructed *Number 98* as well. The same orange-red brick in continuous coursing across the two fronts is tightly laid in black mortar. This brick of smooth surface and even dimension is known as pressed brick, much favored for facing the Greek Revival facades. The recess for the downspout separating the frontage is a subtle refinement.

From Number 98 to West Cedar Street corner

was Jonathan Mason's property. In 1832 Theodore Bowker built *Number 104*. This charmer, diminutive for Greek Revival, is decidedly the runt of the block. In the 1900's it was the home of archetype Brahmin Percival Lowell, whose absolute theory regarding the canals of Mars stirred much astronomical disputation.

By 1837 the building of the block was complete. Before crossing West Cedar Street look back to this row of eight. Subtly and without ambiguity is expressed a quality of variety acknowledging a continuity that is characteristic of Beacon Hill. None of these houses has had benefit of architect. All were built for speculation. No two are identical. Here is an interesting triple dormer — there an odd-sized window — each entrance varies in proportion and detail — a dormer has become a studio window — a mansard has been added — a piece of sidewalk is laid in basket weave. Yet the block reads as consistent architecture.

The pace changes at West Cedar Street. What is left of original building in this block is older and smaller, indicative of hard times of the 1820's. On the south corner the ample but innocuous apartment house touched with Colonial Revival has, perhaps for the best, replaced a Victorian extravaganza. The short block contains no surprises. The few old houses are simple and charming. On the south side *Numbers 112 and 116* were built in 1826, and the house between them a year later. This parcel was owned by Jonathan Mason, who sold it to Cornelius Coolidge, who sold lots to Jesse Shaw, Meshack Tebbets, and George Gibson — all in a trice. The cost of these lots was little more than $1,000. Jesse Shaw, a skillful housewright, probably put up Number 116, lived there, and within the same year built Number 112, "bounded on the east by a ten-foot passage." Meshack Tebbets, bricklayer, built Number 114 the next year. This trio of small Federal town houses illustrates the phrase "conforming individuality." Three-story, brick over granite base, entrance recessed in an elliptical arch, they are of the same genre.

The similar entrances of Number 112 and Number 116 — fanlight flamboyant with matching sidelights framed within a wooden reveal paneled to match stonemasonry — must be the idée fixe of one master builder. The same fan sidelight motif, to a much grander scale, we have observed at Number 90, and we will see it again. Is this feature the architectural imprimatur of Jesse Shaw?

Cross to the north side and peer between the brick sides of what old deeds define as the ten-foot passage. Now Cedar Lane Way, known in the 1870's by the much grander name of Mt. Vernon Avenue, this could be called a Boston mews. Look down at its paving — carefully. The grained brick is wooden. Why, when, how, invite speculation. Wood paving was used for flooring the vast Victorian warehouses. Perhaps an overage was here disposed.

The remainder of the block was developed in 1827, a year after the opposite side, and is a repetition of that scene. The same cast of characters is involved in this. Mount Vernon Proprietor Mason sells parcels to Cornelius Coolidge, who sells lots to Meshack Tebbets, who lays the brick. What remains of the original fronts, certainly *Number 107*, was built by him to his plans. In the deed of sale to William Eaton dated 1827, Meshack Tebbets agrees "to do all carpenter work, painting, glazing, and find all materials in said time for entire completion of two houses with outhouses conformable to plans shown by Tebbets to Eaton." Description continues, "Kitchen 7'-6", roof on pitch one-third covered with boards prepared for slating; suitable lead pipes, tin in front and wood in rear; stairway with hardwood rails and newels; doors and win-

dows in parlors finished with pilaster architraves; folding doors to slide; shutters in parlors
only; all hardware found by Eaton." Built today
to these specifications, the house would be the
same.

Charles Street was once tidewater. The Proprietors, leveling the slopes of Mount Vernon to
take their "brick mansion houses," cut away the
ridge and used the spoil to extend both the banks
of the Charles and their investment. The new
fill provided the street with a strip of embankment. The street began residential and so remained until the end of the last century. Glance
up at the pitched and dormered roofline. One can
discern what is left of the original dwellings. On
Charles Street lived James T. Fields of Ticknor
and Fields, and his admired Annie, who made
their hospitable home a literary salon. Here,
also, resided Massachusetts's Civil War governor, J. A. Andrew, avid abolitionist who financed
the legal defense of John Brown. The Autocrat
of the Breakfast Table, Oliver Wendell Holmes,
was another resident.

First to be attracted west of Charles Street to
this riverbank with its unending potential for
immersion were the Baptists. The zeal with
which they drove their theological wedge into
Boston's Calvinism did not entirely spend itself
in evangelical pursuit. There must have been a
bit of internecine difference in the sharing of the
"old rugged cross." The Second Church broke
away from the First, and the Third broke away
from the Second. "This church, consisting of
nineteen members from the Second Baptist
Church, and of five from the First, was consti-
tuted August 5, 1807. On the same day the
Meeting House was dedicated to the worship of
God." The building is the initial architecture
of Asher Benjamin on Beacon Hill. As with his
later West Church, the plan is square. The cost
of construction was $27,000. Its bell was the

first bell to be used by the Baptist sect in America.

Quoting Longfellow, "I stood on the bridge at midnight, / As the clock was striking the hour," M. A. DeWolfe Howe identified the bell as that in the cupola of the Charles Street Meeting House and the bridge as the predecessor of the present Longfellow Bridge.

The church in its time prospered. Its pastor, the Reverend Daniel Sharp, led his flock with distinction. A Fellow of Brown University and a Harvard Overseer, the Reverend Mr. Sharp was considered by his contemporaries "a perpendicular gentleman of the noblest class." The church, an early proponent of antislavery, welcomed to its pulpit William Lloyd Garrison and Wendell Phillips as well as the Negro leader with that incorruptible name, Sojourner Truth. After the Civil War, with the new terra firma of Back Bay a challenge to home missions, the Baptists recongregated at Clarendon Street and Commonwealth Avenue in solid Richardsonian respectability.

The Charles Street edifice passed in 1867 to the African Methodist Episcopal Church, and here for sixty years this body flourished. In 1920 the street was widened ten feet, and with it (through dedicated effort of architect and neighbor Frank A. Bourne) the Meeting House edged westward. Currently, this important building belongs to the Unitarian-Universalists, who have reactivated the old belfry.

Across the street, in the unmistakable "Sunflower Castle," as it was termed by Holmes, lived Mr. Bourne. To contemporary Hill-dwellers it is as traditional as the Federal and Greek Revival. This house in the early 1900's was the studio-home of an artist, Frank Hill Smith, who may have been responsible for its Bavarianism.

The remaining block is punctuated by the pinnacles of the Church of the Advent. Motivated by the Oxford Movement, the architecture of this church is Boston's best Ruskinesque Gothic, perfectly suited to its beautiful Anglo-Catholic service. Begun in 1878 to plans of John Sturgis, Santayana's kinsman, the structure was completed five years later and to this day remains unchanged. The interior, of the same brick coursed with stone as in the facade, is embellished with and has otherwise absorbed gifts and memorials to have acquired a comfortable worshipped-in character, faintly redolent of frankincense and myrrh.

The Victorian quality of the church seems to have permeated the immediate neighborhood. Solid, eminently respectable, unbeautiful. Like the upper reaches, Mt. Vernon Street west of Charles has had and has its distinguished residents. The Jameses, Henry and William, lived in *Number 131* during the 1860's. More recently, Justice Brandeis lived around the corner on Otis Place. Today Samuel Eliot Morison occupies his grandfather's house on the corner of Brimmer Street, a few houses down the block from that of Boston's mayor.

Mt. Vernon Street ends at Embankment Road. Here, one must brace oneself against the vortex of Storrow Drive traffic. We have roamed the length of Beacon Hill's longest, widest, and shadiest street. Perhaps, again with Henry James, we muse on "the oddity of our nature which makes us still like the places we have known or loved to grow old, when we can scarcely bear it in the people. To walk down Mt. Vernon to Charles was to have a brush with that truth, to recognize at least that we like the sense of age to come, locally, when it comes with the right accompaniments, with the preservations of character and the continuity of tradition, merits I have been admiring on the brow of the eminence."

Chestnut Street

BEACON HILL streets exert a directional tug. One wants to descend Mt. Vernon, go north on Charles, turn south on West Cedar. Pinckney plunges westward into the estuary with the lure of a mirage. Chestnut, however, is an "up" street. Stand on its lower corner and, facing due east, draw a bead on the State House dome framed in red brick. This is cityscape as distinctive as the glimpse of London's St. James's Park through the Horse Guards arcade or the view down Rome's Via Condotti to the backdrop of the Spanish Steps. The Chestnut Street scene is an architectural chronicle of three decades of nascent Beacon Hill — a period when Boston was maturing from a town into a city.

By 1800 the new State House was three years old. The town was recovering from its post-revolutionary austerity, the townsman reasserting his maritime-mercantile leadership. For the next twelve years Boston throbbed with the pulsebeat of expansion. Its population, reckoned at 25,000, for the first time exceeded the prewar figure. Buildings crowded the peninsula, extending the four miles from the Neck to North Battery. These 783 acres contained 2,376 dwellings, eighteen churches, seven schools, four burying grounds, and shores bristling with wharves.

The vision of the Mount Vernon Proprietors when they bought John Singleton Copley's pastures in 1795 had become reality. The virginal acreage of Beacon Hill at turn of the nineteenth century was a realtor's bonanza. In the short interval between 1800 and 1830, Chestnut Street was faced with red brick facades. Today, this street offers the most comprehensive view of domestic Federal architecture in this country.

As Boston grew, the architecture expressed distinctive characteristics, which can be chronologically classified. The first houses located uphill on the eastern slopes are the "mansion houses" — four-storied with dormers, standing free or built in pairs, gracious entrances commanding a wide brick frontage coursed in Flemish bond.

After ten years of brisk activity, the momentum of construction, responding to the economy of the times, stalled in the doldrums created by the Jefferson embargo that led to the War of 1812. When, after some eight years, building resumed, the developer was cautious and square footage of property more costly. The three-story house with an attic became the norm. Tightening of fabric, however, had no effect on quality. The Federal town house of 1819–1829 was constructed, and for the most part designed, with the taste and ability of the master craftsman. Guided by Asher Benjamin's *Builder's Companion*, he produced a regional architecture eminently appealing and, as time has proven, eminently suitable. Look for recurring features of the period as you proceed up the street — particularly for the triple window, a wide central sash framed with side panels. This fenestration, with Palladian refinement, admits maximum light into a narrow interior. The doorway, always a dominant element of the row house, is often arched and deeply recessed to shelter the steps, which vary in number with the slope of the street. The occasional post-lintel opening gives the facade a rectangular character and presages the Greek Revival style of the 1830's. The house invariably rises on a coursing of white

granite, which makes handsome contrast with the red brickwork above and accommodates the pitch of the abutting sidewalk. The gabled slate roofs, framed at a forty-five-degree angle, are usually accented with one dormer or more.

Number 61 is a fine example of the small row house that shows the influence of early Greek Revival, a style which favored a straightforward statement. Its simplicity is accented by the well-proportioned fanlighted doorway. A delicate picked-out detail that trims the head of the doorframe suggests a Benjamin pattern book. The housewright was Bela Stoddard, who bought the land in 1824 for $936 from Jesse Shaw, built the house and lived in it until 1844, when he sold the property for $5,500. Thomas T. Townsend acquired the house in 1854, and it is yet occupied by his descendants. Its simple, substantial neighbor, *Number 59*, continues the brick coursing with identical cornice and a similar arched doorway. It would seem that the two houses were built together, possibly from the plans of Jesse Shaw, another native skilled housewright. Note the frontage laid of a different brick from the side wall — that of a harder burned surface. This change is not unique. The lesser brick was used for party walls.

From here to the West Cedar corner the extended structure, a conversion of two houses, quarters the Harvard Musical Association and contains one of the oldest musical libraries in the country. The east portion was originally the anchor house for the West Cedar block and dates from 1827.

Pause here. The houses on the south side of the street, *Numbers 76 to 70*, were built in 1828 by Cornelius Coolidge, who with Asher Benjamin and Alexander Parris shared Bulfinch's mantle. The Coolidge imprint of arched opening balanced by triple window is the architectural leitmotif of Chestnut and West Cedar Streets.

On the north side of Chestnut Street is a peer group erected within a span of two years. *Number 57* was built in 1828 and has acquired that nebulous identity with Beacon Hill which seems almost like a patina. The brick sidewall is bonded with the granite base of the front to produce a quoined effect that provides a handsome and practical stone corner. The adjoining house, *Number 55,* with the incised stone trim is an 1829 Coolidge. The next two were built by brother housewrights, Benjamin and Howard Bosworth, in 1828. The ancestor of these housewrights was Zaccheus Bosworth, who owned the top of the hill in 1648. Note *Number 53.* The arched window of Palladian inspiration, which occurs in only one other house on the hill (see Number 48), is a Regency refinement. *Number 49,* completed in 1827, and *Number 47* of 1830 are attributed to builders Lee and Leighton. At Number 49 the frivolity of the glass tracery surrounding the door imparts a lively impression. *Numbers 45 to 39,* accredited to the prolific Coolidge, date from 1827 to 1829.

At Willow Street return to the West Cedar Street corner and cross to the south side to find *Number 68.* The next four houses are the work of the successful partnership of Joseph Lincoln and Hezekiah Stoddard. The older houses, *Numbers 64 and 62,* completed in 1817 and 1811, were burned in the great fire of 1824 that consumed the entire lower block of Beacon Street. Within two years they were rebuilt. Stoddard occupied Number 64 and Lincoln lived in Number 62.

Numbers 60 to 50 show once again the admirable architectural efforts of Cornelius Coolidge, abetted financially by John Hubbard. Built in 1824, the six houses are exemplary of the small town house of this period. Here Coolidge is at his best. The deeply recessed barrel-vaulted entrance, trimmed with incised stone banding, embraces the door in a very welcoming gesture. The superimposition of the triple window in decreasing heights as the house rises is indicative of the architect's appreciation of proportion.

Number 52 was acquired in the early 1900's by Ralph Adams Cram, who after years of boardinghouses and a Brookline apartment is quoted, "Perhaps the most salient joy in acquiring the Chestnut Street house was being able to go down into my own cellar, feeling my feet actually on dirt that belonged to me, and for the purpose of getting a bottle of wine, or to see what was the matter with the furnace; or what the cat had brought in!" Mr. Cram, a native of New Hampshire, and his wife, a Virginian, were "by instinct and inclination Beacon Hillites." Indeed, they were to initiate what by now is a fond tradition — the recognition of Christmas Eve with candle-lit windows and roaming carolers. In 1906 the Crams and their guests, as a diversion from an unrewarding attempt "to brew mulled sack out of inappropriate materials," ventured into a cold Christmas Eve to sing "Adeste Fideles" up and down a snowy Chestnut Street. In subsequent years the Chestnut Street Christmas Association distributed handbills, written in beautiful Gothic script, which urged neighbors "to place candles in windows between 6 and 10 to the end that the hearts of passers-by may be gladdened and that Day of Goodwill and Glad Tidings may be fittingly commemorated." Architectural recall of Ralph Adams Cram on Beacon Hill is the interior renovation of the Church of St. John the Evangelist on Bowdoin Street.

A plaque at *Number 50* marks the home from 1863 to 1895 of Francis Parkman, whose histories first accounted North America's development. His arduous expeditions into the wilderness of the northwest to experience in fact his subject matter wracked his never-too-healthy body. Partially blind, arthritis-ridden, he drove himself to the end. Of that quintet of contemporary scholars — Parkman, Prescott, Motley, Ticknor, Bancroft — who from their Beacon Hill libraries introduced the world to American history, Francis Parkman is first among peers.

The house at *Number 48* rewards the close observer. Here the arch of door and arch of window are mated in possibly Beacon Hill's most graceful facade. Even the climbing hydrangea recognizes and defines the delicate propor-

tions. This house is one of the few on Beacon Hill planned for its owner, a Swan daughter who began her married years in another new house on upper Chestnut presented to her by her mother. Mrs. Hepzibah Swan's proclivity for sheltering the distaff members of her family was not limited. Through her agent, William Sullivan, an agreement was negotiated in 1822 with Edward Phillips, who owned the existing house to the east, for use of the "westerly third part of the brick wall . . . as partition wall for building a house. This house to be held in trust for Christiana Keadie Richmond, widow of John T. Sargent, for the yearly rent of one cent." The housewright is not known. Possibly it was Ephraim Marsh, who was very active on this street.

As you pass the next two houses note the Flemish bond, which rarely occurs after 1810. John Howe erected *Number 42* in 1808 and two years later *Number 44* was built by Jeremiah Marsh.

Before reaching the corner of Spruce Street look back to *Number 37*, the complete house of the Federal period. Built after 1824, it represents the best in architectural development of the preceding decades. The rich facade is so well composed that the total effect is understatement. The elaborate wood cornice which extends as head of the fourth-floor windows combines the bracket and fret in an intriguing pattern. The third-floor windows have stone lintels, each with an ornamental key. Below, the piano nobile is expressed with triple guillotine-sash windows opening upon wrought iron balconies. The deep elliptical-arched entrance is defined by incised stone banding broken with floral-carved impost blocks and again the elegant beaded keystone. The three granite steps are contained by quarter round sidepieces. In a finishing grace note the ironwork of the fencing repeats that of the balcony.

Its neighbor with inviting portico (architrave and frieze missing) has a beautiful planted frontage complementary to the facade. Gardens like this one along the north side are a Chestnut Street attraction.

The adjoining comfortable brownstone, a variant of the French Second Empire style, replaces a much older house owned by Benjamin Joy, who at the time of his death in 1828 possessed Numbers 33, 31 and 29. The great mansion at *Number 31* is Greek Revival, fine and pure, but as such is chronologically puzzling. It occupies land purchased in 1800 by Benjamin Joy from the

Proprietorship for $2,400. It is deeded as "8/10ths of a certain piece of land or pasture with 8/10ths of the new house erected and the cellar and materials remaining of the house lately consumed thereon." According to Allen Chamberlain, in 1800 the Mount Vernon Proprietors built as their first venture two separate mansion houses on Chestnut Street at the head of Spruce Street. The house to the east burned. Its site contained the cellar which was incorporated into *Number 29A*. The survivor, *Number 33*, was later refaced in brownstone. Number 31 was erected in the space between the older Joy houses, perhaps in the 1820's.

The house at Number 29A is a Federal mansion house of 1802 origin. Its orientation; its carefully detailed Ionic portico sheltering the arched entrance; its light, restrained ironwork of the balconies identify Bulfinch as the architect. The house has a long and interesting occupancy. In 1809 Gideon Snow bought it for $8,500 from Benjamin Joy. In 1817 it was sold to Charles R. Codman for $7,000. Codman must have added the "swell," which is sensitively joined to the original construction and continues its cornice across the front of Number 31. The brickwork of the bow is American bond and its windows contain the purple glass indicative of the 1820's. A midcentury photograph shows the house painted white. In the place of *Number 29B* was a solarium with glazed arched openings.

Charles Codman's grandson Ogden said that his grandfather bought the white marble urns on either side of the entrance at a Paris auction in about 1830; that they had once adorned the Empress Josephine's chateau, Malmaison. In 1883 the property was purchased by the actor Edwin Booth, who had an enthusiastic Boston following and chose to live among them. Five years later the mansion house passed to a Cambridge educator, John P. Hopkins. Professor Hopkins converted the premises into a boys' high school, adding the wing which is now 29B. Known as "Hoppy's," the school thrived until

the property was sold in 1907. In 1953 the city recognized the converted school wing as an individual dwelling. In 1956 the property was officially divided. The interior contains a winding staircase (a Bulfinch specialty) and handsomely proportioned rooms. Behind the fencing is one of the few unhidden gardens of Beacon Hill.

The adjoining neo-Gothic structure of the 1900's occupies the site of the Ezekiel Hersey Derby House of magnificent repute. Designed as a chapel for the divinity school, subsequently a college of pharmacy at 70 and 72 Mt. Vernon Street, the interior of the chapel was much later converted into condominium units along with the Mt. Vernon Street side of the building.

Cross to the south side again. As you pass *Numbers 28 and 26* note an earlier version of the three-storied row house encountered in the lower blocks. These two houses were built concurrently. The balcony of Number 26 is unusual at first-floor level and is made possible by the steepening grade. The doorway with fan of flamboyant tracery is defined with a deeply articulated egg-and-dart molding (compare with Number 90 Mt. Vernon Street). The twin facades, *Numbers 24 and 22,* feature wooden porticos with, as encountered before, the lower frontal piece of the entablature absent. These houses were built about 1822, possibly by Stoddard and Lincoln.

Numbers 20 and 18 are thoroughly documented. Designed by Cornelius Coolidge in 1823, they were built by Abner Joy, a stonecutter of no relation to Benjamin, who subcontracted the carpentry work to Stoddard and Lincoln. Building specifications exist in the Suffolk County records which define the construction: "In conformity of height and finish to the two houses erected by said Stoddard and Lincoln for Mrs. Swan and Mrs. Howard on said street. Materials to be all of first quality and work done in best manner like the aforesaid houses, except no chimney pieces of wood; pilasters and architraves to the lower story to be like those in Mr. Grant's house on Cambridge Street . . . all done to the entire approbation of Mr. Cornelius Coolidge." It continues further to specify payments of $233 to abutters on either side for use of their wall, and "never to cut more than four inches to fix timbers and to place no timber within four inches of lumber already laid."

As the grade steepens, the height of the roof-line in this block remains continuous, thus reducing *Number 16* to three floors. Such refinement is much appreciated by preservationists for a fine example of street-wall planning. Note the entrance door of two vertical panels. Its simplicity contrasts with the flamboyant tracery of the arched transom. This was Hepzibah Swan's town residence.

East of the passageway, the houses at *Numbers 14 and 12* were also built for house-acquisitive Mrs. Swan. Erected together in 1822 by Stoddard and Lincoln, they too were of Coolidge's design. The arched entrance of Number 14 is Federal at its best. Also fine is Number 12, though the door seems small in the surrounding entrance.

One of the most appealing houses on Chestnut Street is *Number 10*. Small beside its neighbors and simple, its proportions are handled with great precision and its openings carefully balanced. The strongly expressed piano nobile is a dominant horizontal element which gives the illusion of width to the narrow facade.

The handsome adjoining pair came early and are reputedly Bulfinch. In 1804 Charles Paine, son of patriot Robert Treat Paine, built these spacious houses, providing each with side yards wide enough to accommodate a carriage entry. The premises were acquired in 1820 by ubiqui-

tous Cornelius Coolidge, who erected Numbers 10 and 4 in either carriageway. *Number 4* probably was not aligned with Number 10 but extended at a later date, for the present frontage is foreign to Coolidge. *Number 2* at the corner of Walnut Street is a large, heavy house that dates from 1803. Other than for the interesting chimney pots, the neat recessed treatment of the downspout and the warm tone of the brick, this facade is unrelieved simplicity.

Now return half a block to the houses at *Numbers 25 and 23* on the north side. These were twin-built in 1809 by Jeremiah Gardner and have since undergone some renovation. Number 23 presents a proud, high Regency facade that could well adorn London's Adelphi Terrace. Number 25 features a Greek Revival portico with bay — in all probability an 1820's addition.

The two houses next, with ample bows, are late Greek Revival. The "swell" front is a Louisburg Square specialty. On Chestnut Street, this Victorian recall is an architectural stimulant to the older Federal fare.

Beacon Hill's pride are the three town houses of Bulfinch design at *Numbers 13, 15 and 17.* "Daughter houses," they were commissioned by Hepzibah Swan, who was "desirous of limiting and appointing part of premises for advancement of her daughter, Christiana Keadie Swan, free and exempt from control of husband" — so reads the deed of 1806 for Number 13, the first of the three to be built.

In 1807 Number 15 was put up for daughter Sarah's advancement, and in the following year Number 17 was completed for namesake Hepzibah. The deeds also stipulate that, "the stables in the rear will be of such height that the roof be never raised more than thirteen feet above Olive [Mt. Vernon] Street." These are Bulfinch's only extant row houses. Note favorite features from his repertoire: delicately columned en-

trance (see the west portal of Number 45 Beacon
Street); first-floor window recessed in arched
brickwork; piano nobile with light balcony.
Architecture these houses indeed possess, but
here too is a poignant quality of continuity. For
more than a century and a half they have supported and at times seemed to have generated
Beacon Hill life. The Swan daughters, their
descendants and collaterals were alert socially
and intellectually, and their Chestnut Street parlors have a history of hospitality. During the
aftermath of the Civil War, when Boston was
riding its surging philosophical tide, Emerson,
Longfellow, Whittier, Holmes, and other lumi-
naries of the period met regularly for a round
of metaphysics at the Radical Club of Chestnut
Street. Both Numbers 13 and 17 offered hospitality. These houses were homes of Swan
descendants.

For generations the Swans were important to
Chestnut Street. Colonel James Swan, Hepzibah's
husband, is rarely mentioned in documents and
deeds, and when so is "in absentia" or "residing
in Paris." The fact is that he was far from wife-
dominated, as his nonparticipation might suggest. A Scot, he came alone as a youth to America, where he early involved himself in prerevo-
lutionary activity, wrote pamphlets against the
slave trade, attended the Boston Tea Party, vol-
unteered at Bunker Hill, was commissioned and
served in the Continental army. From 1780 to
1781 he was engaged in privateering. The considerable profits of this activity enabled him to
buy the estate of Loyalist Nathaniel Hatch in
Dorchester (where Bulfinch designed a great
mansion for Hepzibah). He negotiated financial
deals with depreciated Continental currency, acquired a loose reputation and consequently found
the climate of France more salutary. In France
he published letters to Lafayette on the causes
of the opposition to commerce between France

and the young republic, attempted to float a loan for two million dollars for the United States from Genoa bankers, aided royalist refugees in fleeing France by shipping their household effects ahead of them. Many of his clients lost their lives as well as their chattels in the Reign of Terror. When their goods arrived in Boston unclaimed, the current witticism was: "The guillotine took their heads, and Swan took their trunks." Eventually imprisoned for debts — he claimed unjustly — Swan was released after many years, only to die shortly thereafter in Paris.

This tale relates to Numbers 17, 15 and 13 Chestnut Street, wherein the French furniture dispatched to Boston by James Swan enhanced drawing and dining room before finding its way to the Boston Museum of Fine Arts to be exhibited as the Swan Collection.

Continuing eastward, we find another Coolidge-Hubbard trio, *Numbers 11, 9, and 7,* built in 1824. These typify the large town house of this period — four stories with attic. The verticality is diminished by the facing of granite, extending from grade to piano nobile, which makes a strong horizontal impression. The design of the facade is expressed with Coolidge finesse, particularly the handling of the openings on the street, where entrance, triple window, and service gate compose an interesting asymmetry.

The twin houses at the corner were built in 1822, together with the original house at *Number 5,* by Ephraim Marsh.

The street ends not far from where the old Copley farmstead fronted the Common. We have found Chestnut Street architecturally laden — its Federal style closely related to that historical period known as the Era of Good Feelings. The ambiance of that era seems yet evident.

West Cedar Street

In Beacon Hill's bucolic past the lower western slopes of Mount Vernon, extending down to Cambridge Bay, so called, comprised two pastures. Land northward was owned by Zachariah Phillips, a butcher, who put his pasture to practical use in support of his livelihood. Abutting on the south in the approximate vicinity of Pinckney Street were the six acres left to William Blaxton after he had sold the remainder of "Tramount Peninsula" to John Winthrop. By the mid–seventeen hundreds a bit of the northern shore land had been laid out in home lots. There was little residential response. The remoteness of this tidal stretch, accessible principally by water, attracted a seafaring clientele whose landside pursuits were to give this part of Beacon Hill the early sobriquet of "Mount Whoredom." Southward, however, the acreage remained pastoral and eventually was acquired by John Singleton Copley as the western addition to his Beacon Hill farmstead. As such it was sold in 1795 to the Mount Vernon Proprietors, who did not get to disposing of it as real estate until some thirty years later.

West Cedar Street is a transection of these two ancient pastures, early developing more or less properly at its south and north extremities. Shown on old maps as George Street, that portion from Myrtle Street south remained a country lane until after 1826, when the Proprietors dissolved their syndicate into individual hold-

ings. This signaled the most ambitious hillside residential project yet undertaken. During the next year John Hubbard, acquiring the entire west block from Chestnut Street to Mt. Vernon, built the row of fine late Federal town houses. Today most of them remain little if at all altered. The ensemble of arched portal and sidelighted window, which recalls the facades of lower Chestnut Street, bears the architectural imprint of Cornelius Coolidge. The parade of doorways, each in some way distinctive, compose as felicitous a continuity of street architecture as exists in Boston. A perspective of this west block from the corner of Mt. Vernon conveys the rhythm of a musical scale. The cornices may be chords, receding in pitch with the slight slope of the street to identify each house.

The east side of this block presents a differing but complementary scene. Here the sequence of brick frontage is cleft by the ten-foot opening into Acorn Street, which irresistibly draws the eye up its cobblestoned ascent.

One first finds Acorn Street with the intimate pleasure of discovering a secret hidden from time. No angular distraction of antennae, no evidence of General Motors, nothing indicates that time has progressed beyond the year of 1828–1829, when this simple row of nine houses was built. In scale with the narrow lane, the south side facades make an easy transition from late Federal to early Greek Revival, each with its own temperament, yet all bearing a family resemblance. Most if not all of the houses were built by Cornelius Coolidge, perhaps for tradesmen and Chestnut Street retainers.

Back on West Cedar Street and observing the remaining east block of houses, we find it obvious that another style confronts us. In 1834, eight years after the houses across the street were put up, *Numbers 7 and 9* were built, and

Number 11 the year following. Boston by this time had embraced the Greek Revival.

The parcel of land had been acquired by Charles Hubbard of Dorchester (no relation to John of the west side), an ornamental painter. In December of 1833 Oliver Downing, a housewright, purchased the corner property at Acorn Street for $959.50. A month earlier, the adjoining lot had been sold to Asher Benjamin for fifty cents more. We assume that Downing built the two houses in 1834, that Number 9, and possibly Number 7, was Benjamin-designed. Both buildings were constructed together and both mortgaged to Charles Hubbard. The architect lived in one, the builder in the other. Since the architect designed Number 9 as his residence, one surmises that he indulged in favorite detail. Indeed, the facade characterizes his expression at this time.

A new sixth edition of Benjamin's *The American Builder's Companion* was published in 1827, introducing the style of Greek Revival to the American practitioner and setting up criteria. Such straightforward virtues of simplicity, strength, boldness, and "massy moldings" are

extolled with the same vaguely defined enthusiasm with which today's critic speaks of integrity,
clarity, brutalism.

The fact is that these houses of the early
thirties are somewhat plainer in appearance, but
vary little in general treatment of fenestration
and overall size from the earlier Federal style.
The unpretentious, structurally obvious post-
and-lintel doorway is the identifying feature of
this transition into Greek Revival. Boston architecture, though hardly a quarter century old as
regional prototype, was already tradition-bound.
The Bulfinch-designed or Bulfinch-inspired
houses of Beacon Hill had an innate refinement
with the elasticity to span a gamut of styles.
Certainly, until as late as the 1850's, the variety
in taste of building found basic conformity in
fine proportion and restraint of frivolity. Excess
was as foreign to Boston architecture of this
early period as it was to the mores of the
Bostonian. The delicacy of elegant cornice, of
slim and tall window, was long-lasting, and the
ornamental detail of anthemion, fan, and palmetto leaf, though of many expressions, was
never incongruous.

For the professionally interested it is reward-
ing to examine well Number 9. Here, there may
be the slight temptation to allude in an architectural connotation to the familiar fable of the
shoemaker's children. Finer and older houses of
the architect we have seen on Beacon Street.
Benjamin, in middle age, may have sought practical comfort — yet with familiar finesse. We
see the portal lintel carved like a fine intaglio,
which illustrates his advice to the stonecutter
that the panel be incised for stronger effect. The
short street window has a Bulfinch recall and
respects the elegant piano nobile. The arabesque
of the ironwork is pure Greek Revival yet unique
with its Adam-like grace.

Carrying over to Number 7, the balcony asserts

kinship. Housewright Downing possessed Number 7 until 1851, when it was sold for $9,075 to James Benjamin, one of the two sons of the architect. His daughter Elizabeth's residence we find in the next block.

Number 11, its ample bay window a balancing element to the flat expanse of the neighboring facades, completes this handsome triad. The three belong together. A year after Benjamin and Downing occupied their houses, this lot was sold to James Garland for $925. Garland was another housewright of much skill if, indeed, he designed his house. The timing and proximity of its construction would claim Benjamin, but the asymmetry and the less subtly proportioned openings are not his wont. This very aspect, however, gives the facade interest and charm. The various elements are in perfect composure, and the gracious bay window suggests the unique legitimacy of being part of the original plan. In 1838 Number 11 passed to Amos Binney for $6,500.

Passing on toward Mt. Vernon Street, do not miss *Number 11A*. This courtway frontage has an intimate domestic quality that invites identity. Possibly of the 1920's and built by Percival Lowell, the astronomer, who owned the house on the Mt. Vernon corner, it quite belongs to this elderly neighborhood. The ailanthus possesses the iron palings with undeniable ownership.

Crossing Mt. Vernon Street, we progress further into the 1830's. The west row picks up the early Greek Revival as consistently as the lower west block expresses the late Federal. Mostly put up by housewrights, the individual houses are variations of the unpretentious, pleasing fronts just examined.

Number 22 has a typical past. The land was acquired from the estate of Proprietor Benjamin Joy in 1831 by Melzar Dunbar "for services rendered in repairing Joy's buildings" at Cornhill Square, plus a cash transaction of $1 per square foot. Melzar Dunbar and his brother Loring were active builder-architects of this era. The house was evidently built for the Dunbar residence. Notable are the handsome interiors which, today unchanged, show professional care of a quality beyond the speculative venture. The moldings have the transitional corner pieces, the square block with the deeply undercut acanthus so indicative of the period. The plan as originally intended provided a downstairs parlor opening with double doors into the dining room. The kitchen was below at rear grade level. This familiar arrangement was not typical for the times. The next house, *Number 24*, has been owned by Wendell Phillips, Boston's ardent abolitionist.

Across the street we again encounter familiar dramatis personae: architect Asher Benjamin, housewright Melzar Dunbar, and Proprietor Harrison Gray Otis. The twin houses at *Numbers 25 and 23* were built on lots possessed by Otis when the Mount Vernon Proprietors claimed individual shares in 1826. Subsequently the lots were sold — Number 25 to painter Horace Dupee in 1830 and Number 23 to Dunbar in 1835. West Cedar frontage had by this time become very desirable, and Dunbar paid Otis $2,340. Also in 1835 Asher Benjamin bought Dupee's plot for $1,380.50 (this lot is not so deep as Number 23).

During the next year the Benjamin-Dunbar team put up the two houses. The change of treatment within the brief span of several years is noticeable. The fronts are quite straightforward. The commanding element is the floor-length windows of the first floor, raised above the street sufficiently to provide ample basement window wells. The row of tall windows is given more importance by the continuous iron balcony of bold palmetto pattern, which unifies the two facades. The facades repeat an identical image with very spacious effect. The architecture is simple but not ordinary and probably of Benjamin's design. The architect owned the premises at Number 25 during his lifetime, and at his death in 1845 the property was inherited by his daughter, Mrs. Elizabeth A. Bliss. Dunbar's house was also retained in the family and was sold in 1868 by the estate for $14,000.

The adjoining pair of fine, arched-doorway houses, *Numbers 27 and 29*, have a distinctly Federal character. This is indicative of the early Beacon Hill respect for tradition, for they were erected at a time of initial enthusiasm for the Benjamin-espoused Greek Revival. Referring again to the Division Deed of 1826, we find Proprietor William Sullivan acquiring these lots. He sold Number 27 in 1830 to the housewrights Bela Stoddard and Micah Cutler, in consideration of "work done on fourth house on Western Avenue paid by Bela Stoddard and Micah Cutler, housewrights, who were employed to do the said work," and for the cash amount of $1,111.20. The housewrights capitalized their investment four years later in an arrangement with Theodore Baker, contracting to build a house with the sale of the property to him.

This deal coincided with the construction on the adjacent lot of Number 29. At this point we backtrack to William Sullivan's interest in this parcel, which he held as trustee for the estate of Hepzibah Swan, the only Mount Vernon Proprietress. The lot was inherited by Mrs. Swan's daughter, Hepzibah C. Howard, a real estate dabbler herself, who sold it for $800 in 1833 to Seth L. Thomas. In the transaction of the following year Thomas realized $200 on his investment when the property passed to Grenville Winthrop. Another year later Winthrop sold the land to Abijah S. Johnson, carpenter. This multiplicity of dates and figures and owners illustrates the odds against accuracy in any factual assertion regarding Beacon Hill's architectural past.

These many pieces are fitted together as a supposition that the two houses were constructed from August through November of 1834. Stoddard and Cutler built Number 27 and, most probably, Number 29, which its owner, Abijah S. Johnson, worked on as carpenter. Upon completion of Number 29, the premises were promptly acquired for $5,000 by Wilthea Windsor, for whom the house may have been designed.

Directly across the street is a very different sort of house, possibly the oldest on West Cedar. The neat facade of *Number 36* has a "just-growed," Topsy-like air, belying the fact that architect Cornelius Coolidge made it. The exterior with its guileless charm remains as originally put together in 1828, except for the studding of iron stars, which adds a happy, ingenuous accent. These hexagrams occurring at the second- and third-floor levels are the caps of metal tie rods, devices inserted at a later date to reinforce the structure. When the house was completed, Coolidge sold it for $1,500 to Dr.

George Parkman. Evidently, Dr. Parkman knew a bargain when he saw it — until he met Professor Webster.

On the northwest corner of Pinckney and West Cedar Streets the large house, *Number 42*, marks the beginning of another decade in the development of the street. There is much architectural interest in this severely simple front. One first notes the uncommon framing of the roof. The front wall terminates in a gable, the apex of which is broken very oddly by a central chimney. This roof construction is determined by the slight curvature of the front wall. Why the curvature is an intriguing query. From the entrance on the West Cedar facade, the south portion of the house veers very slightly with the parallel of the street curbing. Nothing in the deed would require it to do so, nor is it a Yankee characteristic to be so profligate with square footage. Whatever the reason, the effect is most graceful.

This corner land belonged to Proprietor Jonathan Mason, whose estate sold it to Benjamin Rogers in 1841 for $833.75. Coincidentally, Rogers acquired the abutting ten-by-twelve-foot patch on the north and erected the house. The lower wing that fills this small plot is a later addition. The first sale of the premises was in 1869 for $10,000.

From here to Cambridge Street the scale of the block changes. The houses, of smaller, narrower fronts, make up the remainder of this block, which was built up by 1850. Housewright Oliver Downing and land owner Kirk Boot were very active in the Pinckney-to-Revere-Street block. As the houses get smaller the street scene gains individuality. This end of West Cedar Street is not architecturally nor historically of great note. However, it teems with activity, providing a lively counterbalance to West Cedar's proper, southern extremity.

Pinckney Street

It is claimed for Pinckney Street, particularly on a summer's day when white sails crowd the river, that it offers Boston's most spectacular view. At a vantage up from Anderson Street (originally the crest of Mount Vernon), the sight of the Charles drops into complete perspective. In the opposite direction, a less dramatic yet fine cityscape is the sight due east from the lower slopes leading directly up to the Custom House tower, which fills the narrow horizon.

It is further claimed for Pinckney Street that its character is more noteworthy than its architecture — that it composes in abbreviated bits all the aspects that make up the feel of Beacon Hill. The course of its steep stretch, beginning

a hundred yards north of the State House dome and plummeting into the river, runs the gamut of Beacon Hill domesticity from eighteenth century wooden cottage through proper Greek Revival to current multiapartment units. Here unfolds a historic panorama full of fact, fiction and lore.

Before Pinckney Street existed, there were dwellings on the eastern heights. The land was the pasture of Elisha Cooke, Jr., who in 1730 parceled it into lots. An approach, which was laid out straight and steep from Cambridge Street, was first known as Clapboard Street. (This is now Joy Street, off which a "new street," so called in property deeds of 1800, led westward to the building sites.) The "new street" was named in 1802 in commemoration of a Southern patriot and statesman, Charles Cotesworth Pinckney, who like Patrick Henry, made the schoolboy's primer for generations with a phrase, "Millions for defense but not one cent for tribute!" Whether or not this gambit was ever directed to Talleyrand during the republic's early negotiations with France, it has a proud ring. Pinckney, as vice-presidential candidate, shared John Adams's defeat in the United States' fourth election. Such circumstances may have prompted the legislature to honor a fellow Federalist who is the only non-Yankee, other than George Washington, with a Boston street to his credit.

One of the earliest purchasers of the younger Elisha Cooke's pasture was Temple Decoster, housewright, who acquired the northwest corner in 1735. This twenty-five-foot-by-seventy-five-foot rectangle with narrow side on Clapboard Street was left undisturbed for the next fifty years. In 1786 Decoster's children sold their hilltop inheritance to Louis Clapion and George Middleton. The pair, presumably bachelor friends, jointly built the small house that is now

Number 5. The little wooden house seems much too innocent for all the documentation spent on its identity. But to the antiquarian, it is a leading contender for the oldest house on Beacon Hill. No one disputes its charm, and timeless simplicity gives it a changeless presence. Yet at some period during its younger years it lost ten feet or more of house.

Early tax records describe it as wooden, one-story, four windows (the number of windows establishes the value of $600). Clapion was a French mulatto, hairdresser by occupation, and his housemate, Middleton, a black man with the trade of "horsebreaker." Barber and liveryman seem to have got on well enough until Clapion married. Shortly thereafter, in 1792, a division of ownership was deeded, and the property, referred to as a "certain tenement and messuage of land," was parted right down the middle with each possessing a moiety of house and side yards.

During the next thirty-five years documents become so entangled with changes of ownership, mortgages and foreclosures, dower claims, and deed discrepancies that accurate account is, at best, conjecture. We pick up the factual trail again in 1827. The wooden house, then numbered 5 and 7, was owned by a cobbler, William Younger, who used it as residence and shop — each with its entrance. By some quirk of circumstance the premises have possessed an attraction to shoemakers. Succeeding in 1831 was Alexander H. Clapp, who here lived and cobbled until 1838. Joseph K. Adams, custom booter, next made it home and shop. The Adams family occupied the place for fifty-three years.

Though the north side of Pinckney was built up almost coincidental with the grading of the street, construction opposite was sparse and entirely related to the great mansions facing Mt. Vernon Street. For many years the south extent of Pinckney Street was a definition of backyards.

Before starting downhill, notice the gray-painted houses facing Joy. They are very old, having been built by Stephen Higginson in 1803. The brick coursing is in Flemish bond. The bay window and Greek Revival balcony are later additions.

Cross to the north walk. *Numbers 9 and 11* are latecomers for this end of the street. They were put up in 1824 by Benjamin Russell, a publisher who was active in speculative real estate. There is architectural merit to this pair. Twin-built, the houses repeat in mirror image the same facade, to appear as a unified composition. This treatment, which gives a spacious symmetry to the two fronts, is peculiar to Beacon Hill. The entrance of Number 9, and originally Number 11, with the arched transom of flamboyant tracery, is one of the half dozen of this design on the hill. The others are Numbers 90, 112, and 116 Mt. Vernon, 16 and 26 Chestnut, 7 Charles: all built in the 1820's.

Upper Pinckney Street early attracted the litterateur. *Number 9* was the home in the late 1830's of an important American educator of music and composer of hymns, Lowell Mason. At *Number 11* lived Edwin P. Whipple, a literary critic popular in the decades that followed the Civil War. Whipple gave the high end of Pinckney a certain social distinction. His "Sunday evenings" were eagerly attended by the Boston intelligentsia. More recently, from about 1904 to the end of the 1940's, this was the home of Pinckney Street's most successful novelist, Alice Brown, who won the Winthrop Ames prize of $10,000 in 1915 for *Children of the Earth.*

On the south side at *Number 4*, the former site of a stable, lived Jacob Abbott, author of the *Rollo* books and progenitor of the Horatio Alger series *Born to Succeed.*

The wide frontage at *Number 15* has an institutional aspect. Indeed, it served as a private hospital for some time before the First World War. Its construction as apartment building in 1895 absorbed an open court, along with a house facing east upon it which was a reverse duplicate of *Number 17* and built at the same time.

Number 17 is very old and a veteran of many face-liftings. In 1798 Joseph Carnes, Jr., a ropemaker, and Daniel Stainford, a schoolmaster, acquired a parcel of eight lots on the "new street." The lots sold quickly, and by 1800 a house fronting a courtyard occupied Number 17. That very year the new premises were sold at auction by Suzanna Wood, whose late husband Robert Wood, a housewright, had built the house. The highest bid for "land with dwelling thereon standing" was $1,375 from James Otis, another housewright. The original structure, brick firewalls parallel with neighboring property lines and containing end walls of timber, represents the economical construction of this period. In 1856 the property was sold to Gridley J. F. Bryant, whose father, Gridley Bryant, was a self-educated engineer. The elder Bryant's important contribution to the building of New England was the device for transporting Quincy granite: a gravity-energized railway which, restrained by horses, conveyed huge slabs from the mountainside quarry down to Quincy Point. From here it was barged up and down the Atlantic coast, a considerable tonnage unloaded in Boston. Gridley J. F. Bryant, with bold technique and expansive scale, so disposed the large stones his father's railroad brought him to become Boston's most successful architect of the post–Civil War era. He was referred to by critics as a stabilizing force, and that he was! However, wood as a building material was not his métier. We attribute to Bryant the accumulation of heavy Victorian details that Number 17 now supports — bracketed cornices, quoins, and architraved lintels. Nor is the handsome entrance original;

arched, Federal, and appropriate though it is. This doorway replaced within the last ten years an earlier replacement of an ornately canopied Victorian porch. In 1870 Bryant sold the property for $16,000. The off-street orientation is significant. Bulfinch planned mansion houses on Mt. Vernon and Chestnut streets in this fashion.

On the south side, in about 1827, Jonathan Mason began to reassess the peripheral reaches of his great Mount Vernon estate. He divided the Pinckney frontage of his backyard into small building lots, which extended from Number 12 to 38. The first sale was to Frederick Hughes, a tailor, who built two houses, *Numbers 18 and 20*. In the backyard of Number 18 a fine well supplied fresh water. The next year, 1828, Ebenezer Nichols built *Number 16* and was permitted to share the water supply of the adjoining house if he provided an access through his own property from the street to the well. This is the narrow passage under Number 16, which was used by Hughes for his convenience but was restricted to others for watering purposes only.

In the present century, between World Wars, Number 16 housed the Boston-loved poet Louise Imogen Guiney. Also, Edwin Munroe Bacon, journalist and connoisseur of historical and literary New England, has lived here.

The facade of *Number 20* has a friendly architectural countenance. Unpretentious and intimate in scale, this small house seems an appropriate home for a child. Young Louisa May Alcott lived here when the family was struggling with the ineptness of Bronson Alcott as paterfamilias.

Jonathan Mason's final sale before his demise was made in 1830 to that familiar duo, housewrights Joseph Lincoln and Hezekiah Stoddard, who built Numbers 12 and 14. Joseph Lincoln moved from the house he had built and lived in on lower Chestnut to Number 12 at the top

of Pinckney, where his family resided for generations.

Number 22 was put up in 1838, possibly by
Cornelius Coolidge (there is no Beacon Hill street
without a Coolidge). He acquired this property
with the 57 Mt. Vernon Street house and sold
it forthwith to Amos Binney, a navy agent. A
proviso specified that a three-story brick house
be built according to approved plans.

The adjoining house, *Number 24*, is the most
architecturally interesting of Pinckney Street's
frontages. The building is far older than its
William Morris individualism would imply.
What is left of the original structure, possibly
only its size and a few square feet of brick
masonry, is Jonathan Mason's stable, built with
the Mt. Vernon Street mansion in 1802.

Chamberlain recounts that during Mason's
lifetime the stable was adapted to a grocery store
serving successive proprietors as such for over
a decade. When the Mason estate was divided
in 1836, the Pinckney Street stable was part of
the parcel which included the carriage court of
the Mt. Vernon Street mansion house. The next
year a new house at Number 59 Mt. Vernon
Street covered the erstwhile carriage court, and
the street-to-street property has never been divided. The Mt. Vernon Street house became the
home of Thomas Bailey Aldrich before the turn
of the century, when the Pinckney Street stable-
grocery store was remodeled in about 1884 as
a town house. The architect, William Ralph
Emerson, a cousin of Ralph Waldo Emerson,
was prominent in the building of the Back Bay.
The architecture, if classifiable, may be included
with that accumulation of vagaries which in the
1880's the English innovators referred to as
Queen Anne. Although eccentric — of its many
windows no two are the same size — and out of
time — there is a picturesque medievalism about
the asymmetric massing — yet the shapes and

sizes do compose, and the design has balance. Were the lintels of the first-floor windows in line with the lintels of the doors, the proportion would be more refined, but, in current parlance, the architect made his statement — and it has endured.

Next to please us is the meandering, emphatic brick frontage of *Numbers 34 and 36*. The great arched portal sheltering the flight of entry steps is pure Richardsonian — a lesser variation of the entrance treatment at Trinity's rectory in Back Bay.

The heavy stone banding, the odd-sized but organized fenestration are all here. The gateway, Number 34, with the name Warren on the metal escutcheon probably led to the service entrance of Number 67 Mt. Vernon Street, which Samuel D. Warren owned in the 1870's. Warren must have put up this early apartment venture, designed as such by a protégé of the busy Richardson atelier in Brookline.

The houses westward to the alley make up a neighborly block. The pleasing, latter-day colonial front of *Number 38* is the most recent. *Number 46* is the oldest in this group and can be found on surveys dated 1832. Unaltered are *Number 40* and *Number 46*. Less than ten years ago *Number 44* was fronted with a two-story bay window of weighty Victorian vintage, which projected menacingly over the sidewalk at a height of five feet. The replacement is in plane with the adjoining facades if not of the repetitive brick.

Look to the other side where the ailanthus tree reaches across from the court of *Number 47*. Confronting us is housewright-Federal at its best. Built in pair, Numbers 47 and 49 are the joint efforts of Jeremiah Gardner, carpenter, and Peter Osgood, bricklayer. In 1804, each paying the other one dollar, Gardner possessed "a dwelling house being the easterly part of a new, double brick dwelling house," and likewise Osgood assumed ownership of the westerly house. The exterior of Number 47 is unchanged since Osgood laid the brick and Gardner installed the fine Georgian entrance. Note the elegant guilloche cornice of molded brick — it can be found on the Bulfinch houses at Numbers 55 and 57 Mt. Vernon Street, built in the same year.

The adjoining houses, *Numbers 51 and 53*, were constructed together, though not as a pair. Built in the first decade of the 1800's, they were simple and practical of design. Over the past century and three-quarters each has responded to refinements, and now their appearance is quite individual. The interiors are spacious, and each possesses a fine rear garden. At *Number 55* the old fabric has received much care and today presents the neat, clean aspect of a new house, belying its one hundred and seventy years. From here to the corner the narrow vertical houses are typical of the vernacular row house at the turn of the century. The three tall structures nearest the corner are severely functional. They were built by 1807. The cupola of *Number 65* once provided a comprehensive view of the anchorage directly below the hill along the north waterfront. This building was put up by shipowners to afford housing for sailors waiting to be shipped on another China trader. Its roominghouse character yet prevails.

On the south side the houses from *Numbers 48 to 56* were built in the early 1830's and originally were three-story dormered structures expressing a simple dignity in plain, well-proportioned facades. Bay windows and upper stories came later. *Number 54* is the only building in the row to remain untouched. George Hillard, transcendentalist, man of letters, scholar, publisher, law partner of Charles Sumner, close friend of Nathaniel Hawthorne, occupied this house in the 1840's before building his own a few steps farther down the street. Under this roof he befriended the near-destitute author on his return from the Brook Farm Colony. Hawthorne penned a note from Number 54 requesting a minister to wed him to Sophia Peabody. The message omitted the day and place, though it mentioned "Unless it should be a decidedly rainy day, a carriage will call for you at half past eleven oclock in the forenoon." The marriage occurred in Elizabeth Peabody's bookshop on West Street.

Later, Hillard published an account of a visit to Italy when Hawthorne was American consul at Rome. Entitled *Six Months in Italy*, the diary became a guide for generations of tourists.

Number 56 was built in 1833 by William Snow, a painter. For its period and for so modest a house, the entrance has an earlier, elaborate Federal recall. The eighteen-foot street frontage is tight but not uncommon; however, the west party wall veers eastward to the extent that the rear of the house is barely seven feet wide — thus its sobriquet, "Pie House."

At Anderson Street the view down the north slope closes on the classic facade of Bulfinch's Massachusetts General Hospital. When it was built in 1821 on the true banks of the Charles, patients could arrive by boat.

The commanding building on the west corner of Anderson Street was Beacon Hill's first schoolhouse, built in 1820 for English High School. The curriculum was structured for "lads intending to become merchants or mechanics." The edifice has architectural quality. The plan, a Greek cruciform, is quite suited to its square plot. An early photograph shows a light, airy octagonal cupola rising about the roof. The arched recesses that frame tall second-floor windows and the stone banding that defines the floor levels are Federal in style. The heavy Doric entrance, however, is pure Greek Revival.

Westward from Anderson Street to West Cedar Street, the north block of houses came with the next decade, as did most of the building on the south side. The extent of Pinckney Street frontage from *Numbers 58 to 66* was the backyard of Harrison Gray Otis's mansion on Mt. Vernon until 1845, when the estate was acquired by Samuel Hooper, a speculator. Within several months five sizable lots were on the market. Gridley J. F. Bryant, encountered at Number 17, advised Hooper in subdividing the land and probably designed the houses built by Hooper for prospective buyers. This would represent Bryant's earliest residential work. (His row on Commonwealth Avenue, Numbers 20 to 36, is of the Civil War era and features the mansard roof, a Second Empire motif which Bryant introduced to Boston.)

Number 58 was built to the Victorian criterion of solid comfort. Its exuberant bay window, original to the house, is a curiosity in copper and glass. The house was first acquired by James Freeman Clarke, pastor of the Church of the New Disciples.

Number 62 was bought by George Hillard, former resident of Number 54. This Pinckney Street house may have been the station "above suspicion" on Boston's underground railroad. Other than Mrs. Hillard's enthusiastic abolitionism, facts are unverified.

The last of this genre, *Number 66,* is the most appealing architecturally. The two-panel door with its beautiful old brass is colonial of character. The granite substructure and the ironwork are fine Greek Revival. Residentially, the house is even more significant. It offered hospitality to the disillusioned of the Brook Farm commune when that notable pre-Marxian experiment collapsed. Among the Brook Farmers was John Sullivan Dwight, who lived here a number of years and, like neighbor Hillard, was a man of many facets. An intellectual, Unitarian minister, German scholar, poet, Dwight made his most important contribution as a music critic and publisher of the *Journal of Music*. The house since 1921 has been the home of Catharine Sargent Huntington of Thespian renown. Miss Huntington has promoted theater in Boston since the dramatic days of the *Boston Stage Society* in the 1920's and was cofounder of the *Provincetown Playhouse on the Wharf,* producing O'Neill's plays from 1940 for over thirty years.

A few doors down the slope is *Number 74.* To the local chronicler frustrated at lack of identity other than hearsay, this small house — original to the color of its front door — tells all. Here is the completely documented domestic construction of Beacon Hill. Architect John Kutts drew plans, and the house was erected in 1829 to detailed specifications by Phineas Weeks and Amos Perrin. Nine months was the stipulated building time; the contractors to furnish all materials; marble chimneypieces in the parlor to be worth from $90 to $100 a pair; three coats of lead and oil paint for interior woodwork; wallpaper to cost up to $1 a roll. Specified also were the brick sidewalk with granite edgestones, a cistern, pump, and twelve-gallon copper boiler. Compensation for the complete project was to be $2,900 plus a rear plot of 1,856 square feet subject to a mortgage of $400. The first owner was David Chapin. Now it is the home of Marjorie Drake Ross, Boston historian.

The rear lot, part payment for construction of Number 74, the contractors sold to fellow housewrights Joshua and Benjamin Turner in 1831 for $933. By 1834 there was a house on the property assessed to Joshua Turner, who had leased it to Thomas Haskins, a hardware dealer. This is the hidden house of Beacon Hill, *Number 74½.* Approached only from a passageway through the front building, the house is completely self-contained and possesses a bit of a southern garden, all entirely walled in by the surrounding brick dwellings. Number 74½ is a sanctum of charm as well as of privacy, and has for years been the home of the John Codmans. Mr. Codman is credited for his activities in establishing legal protection for the architecture of Beacon Hill.

The next pair, *Numbers 76 and 78*, are small but boldly stated. These swell-fronted facades compose the most intimate Greek Revival in Boston where one may live unpressured by the Olympian complex. Loring Dunbar and Samuel Mitchell were the housewrights and sold both properties to Joshua Bennett, an active speculator from Billerica and possibly a first absentee landlord.

Beyond the sheer wall of St. Margaret's Convent we become aware that the street broadens into Louisburg Square. No such spatial interlude is even suggested by the view from either end, down or up this straight street. However familiar the Hill-dweller is with this expanding scene, he is pleasantly diverted by it. Pause at the corner and look over to the north frontage. The balconied facades completing the quadrangle are, though slightly smaller, of the same Greek Revival family as the houses on either side of the square and of the same age.

The decade of the 1830's saw a surge of new building which, centered in Louisburg Square, reached up and down Pinckney Street. The economy was recovering from the panic of 1829. Even more stimulating to the sluggish real estate market was rumor of imminent settlement of the prolonged title dispute over the lands of lower Pinckney Street. The Overseers of the Poor contended prior rights to a pasture of the Copley farmstead. The Proprietors' claim was to prevail.

Until 1834 the entire parcel from West Cedar Street to Louisburg Square was untouched. The land had been divided into lots of individual ownership in 1826, but no further activity ensued. In 1834 the Proprietors set to, each developing his own. Pinckney Street filled rapidly from the square to West Cedar Street and on the north side all the way up to the schoolhouse at Anderson Street. Carpenters and builders by the 1840's clustered in small shops about the bottom of the hill. At least fifteen local housewrights were at work. Most active were Jesse Shaw at the corner of Charles and Pinckney Streets and Oliver Downing at a Charles Street address opposite the Meeting House. That their efforts were good, time has attested. Look down the street and observe that the converging perspective of brick frontages composes here, as on Mt. Vernon Street, a theme of many variations. Top floor or extra dormer may be added, Victorian bay cantilevered over the brick walk and possibly a lintel lifted for an arched doorway, yet these buildings are complementary and should be appreciated en masse.

The lower slope of the street also has its interesting lore. The plain, neat corner house facing West Cedar Street and its adjoining Pinckney Street neighbor of the gracious fanlighted doorway, *Number 86,* seem rather to ignore each other. The fact is their floor plans are locked together. The basement of one extends beneath the street floor of the other, and a closet or so veers beyond the party wall. This came about by the insistence of the builder of the two houses that his progeny inheriting the property live next to each other, bonded by more than family ties.

A notable resident of this block was Thomas Bailey Aldrich, editor of *The Atlantic Monthly* before the 1900's and luminary of the Boston literary scene. Though not native-born, he claimed to be "Boston-plated." His bridal home in 1866 was "the quaint little house 84 Pinckney

Street," according to his bride. Here, the next year, Dickens was entertained. Again quoting the bride, "Turning to me he said, 'Now I want to see this wonderful house from top to bottom, from cellar to attic!' " Nor was Longfellow far behind. Again from the bride, "After a half hour's friendly chat of books and men, Mr. Longfellow said, 'May I tell you how I am impressed with the atmosphere of home and cheer you have given to this little room? Its crimson walls, the flowers, the crowded shelves of books, all tell their story of the fortunate, the happy day, when a new household found its place among the innumerable homes of earth.' " Thus inspired, it is intimated, the poet home composed "The Hanging of the Crane."

The next short block leads us down to Charles Street and across into the more recent past. This is filled land, and we may in fact be treading the crests of Mount Vernon and Beacon Hill. The trim row of fine Victorian brickwork on the south seems an overflow from Brimmer Street. On the north the view-oriented apartment building, River House, is postbellum World War Two and said by the native to be designed by "New York architects."

We come to the river, blessedly free of a pedestrian overpass leading to its shoreside park. Indeed, such was considered in the 1950's to be warded off by the vigilant efforts of the Beacon Hill Civic Association. On the curb of Storrow Drive the ramble down Pinckney Street is obviously at its end — except to recount a last item for the memorabilia collector. On top of the hill at Number 15 — the original house is long since replaced — there was for seven years in the 1860's a small school. Here Elizabeth Peabody, "Miss Birdseye" in Henry James's *Bostonians*, conducted one of America's first kindergartens. She taught not in vain. The nursery school is a Beacon Hill institution.

Louisburg Square

I~N~ REGARD~ to Louisburg Square, the notion of quality is more pervasive than that of locale. The suggestion of integrity and decorum and style is a reflex — the impression of red brick and cobblestone and elm tree is an afterimage.

What prompts this emotional response to less than a quarter of an acre of sloping terrain defined by a rectangle of thirty-one period houses? Its historical impact is nil; there is older and better architecture on the hill; the Dutch elm disease has wreaked devastation upon the trees; the drive is rough with potholes; the statuary has doubled as ballast.

The common denominator may be that Louisburg Square appeals to the psyche. A person identifies with the intimate, open space so responsive to the four seasons. He senses the harmony in the repetitive facades — solid, unpretentious, and friendly.

The square may have had its origin in a Bulfinch concept of 1796. In S. P. Fuller's map of 1826 the square was moved westward, much reduced in size, and turned ninety degrees on its longitudinal axis. This is the open space as we now know it. Fuller made his survey to accompany an indenture that defined streets and lots and distributed ownership to the remaining four of the Mount Vernon Proprietors: Harrison Gray Otis, Jonathan Mason, Benjamin Joy, and William Sullivan.

"Louisburg" was first named on this map and

so spelled. There is reason to believe that the
name commemorates the victory of the Massachusetts colonials who had captured the impreg-
nable French-Canadian fortress of Louisbourg in
1745. The expedition was identified with Boston,
from whence it sailed for Cape Breton with
some three thousand men led by the president
of the Governor's Council, William Pepperell.
It is said, without verification, that a grandson
of William Blaxton, Boston's first resident, fell
at the siege.

Eight years after being created on paper by
deed of indenture, the square began to take
shape in fact. In 1834 the lots found buyers, and
the buyers built houses. The first built was at
Number 19 on the upper corner at Pinckney
Street. The lot sold for $2,092. It has been
renovated with the three original adjacent houses
for St. Margaret's Convent, an Anglican order.
Before becoming a convent, in 1860 Number 19
was the scene of Mayor Frederick Lincoln's
levee honoring the Prince of Wales. Edward
VII, then nineteen, was more Boston-feted than
Lafayette had been. Mayor Lincoln invited thirty
guests to his Louisburg Square home. It was re-
ported that "Mrs. Henry W. Longfellow looked
queenly in a scarlet velvet headdress with a
white plume going half round to the front of
her head."

On the opposite corner of Pinckney, the lot at
Number 22 was bought by Jesse Shaw the housewright in 1835 for $2,936. He built the house
in the same year and sold the premises for
$14,500, an appropriate price for the time. The
house at *Number 8* was built in 1835 by Phineas
Upham and sold for $14,500 to Andrew Fearing
and his wife of the interminable name, Aldeber-
ontophoscophornia. The next year the premises
went for $15,250. Other houses to appear in
1835 were *Numbers 10 and 12* west and *Numbers 7 and 9* east. The Swedenborgians found

the high side of the square to their liking. Number 7 was built by an early doctrinaire whose son became pastor of the Church of the New Jerusalem, and the neighbor at Number 9 was the first Swedenborgian minister in Boston.

Added to the lower side in 1836 were *Numbers 14 to 20* and to the upper side *Numbers 11 to 17*. The south ends of the two sides of the square were the last to be built up. The proximity to Mt. Vernon Street may have been a value factor, hence the more costly property.

Numbers 4 and 6 were erected by Jesse Shaw. In 1842 he bought the land from the Mason estate for $6,403.93. The parcel, with frontage of 36'9", consisted of Lot Number 4 and half of Lot Number 6 as laid out on Fuller's plan. The divided property had been jointly owned by Otis and Mason. The new house at Number 6 was sold to Samuel Neal. Shaw retained Number 4 and perhaps lived there until 1857, when Charles Mason, Jonathan's son, bought the property for $18,000.

By 1842 Numbers 4, 5 and 6 were constructed. Five years later *Numbers 1, 2 and 3* filled the gaps, and the open space was walled with brick facades.

The new homeowners, house-proud and forming a neighborhood, gathered at Number 19 in 1844 for considering means to "enlarge and adorn said square for the mutual advantage and enjoyment of said parties being such owners." The meeting was historical. It resulted in the organization of the Proprietors of Louisburg Square, which has become the prototype for civic groups throughout the country. Membership included owners "of dwelling houses thereon bounding on Easterly, Westerly, and Northerly sides of Louisburg Square in said city." "Northerly" refers to Numbers 79 through 91 on Pinckney Street, which make up that end of the square. At the southern end, the houses

on Mt. Vernon Street, built earlier, were not included. Basically, the agreement pledged responsibility of houseowner and heir to "pay an equal proportion of expenses of keeping in repair and embellishing the ground enclosed within said Square." Possession of the mall with its bordering side streets was established exempt from city control. Covenants assured that Louisburg Square be extended and enlarged. A modus operandi was set up, and all was declared in perpetuity. Today, this agreement functions within the original concept. It was signed by twenty-two neighbors. The tangible benefits were soon to be realized. The "grass area" was extended by ten feet and widened by eight feet. A handsome iron fence was erected, and the *Ulmus americana* planted. The fence was of a proper Victorian sturdiness and cost $6,000. The statuary came shortly thereafter.

A new resident who was an affluent Mediterranean merchant as well as Turkish consul, Joseph Iasigi, occupied Number 3. Moved by beneficence or, as is facetiously recounted, in search of a depository for the stone ballast from the hold of his ship, Iasigi asked the Proprietors to receive, gratis, Aristides the Just as "embellishment for the grass area." A year later, 1850, Aristides rose on his pedestal and at the opposite end of the green, Columbus as well — who, indeed, could claim proprietary rights. On close inspection the two statues appear to be, if not from the same chisel, from the same school. These objects were turned out in mid–nineteenth century Italy in production-line quantity — slightly under life-size, serene of countenance and pose. How one recognizes the himation-draped figure as that of Aristides we may well ask. The globe at Columbus's knee is, at least, clue to his identity.

With all the enthusiasm for landscaping, a Victorian fountain was inevitable. However, its

tenure midway between Columbus and Aristides
was brief. In 1850, the fountain was installed.
Six years later, it was replaced with a flower
bed. During that interval it was caught in full
spray by the house artist of *Gleason's Pictorial
Drawing Room Companion*. This print, depicting
a somewhat lugubrious Columbus with the fountain erupting over his shoulder, is found in many
Beacon Hill reception halls.

Architecturally, the houses of Louisburg
Square have been acclaimed the finest row of
Greek Revival in New England. Nowhere else
in Boston, even in the expanse of Back Bay, is
the identity of a period so accurately captured
and preserved. The lower row from Number 8
to Number 22 shows an imaginative affinity for
the sloping site unusual to the conformity of this
style. The entrance floor is elevated to provide
a basement areaway accommodating full windows and a service access. The simple granite
stoop of open steps and slab is deftly fitted and
balanced. The piano nobile is on the first floor
just at eye height to afford an irresistible glimpse
of fine mahogany and Georgian silver. Asher
Benjamin may have introduced this sophisticated
play of levels first found in his granite houses,
Numbers 70–75 Beacon Street, and in the twin
houses at Numbers 23–25 West Cedar Street.
The proportions of this three-story row are of a
very pleasing domestic scale. Here and there is
a distinctively beautiful detail. See the front door
of *Number 14* with the lotus-carved panels, the
Doric portico at *Number 8*, and the conelike sky-
lights projecting from the rooftops discernible
from the upper sidewalk.

From the time of their building, these houses
have supported a gracious life-style. In recent
years Christmas Eve in Louisburg Square has
been celebrated as a social prelude to the reli-
gious celebration at the Church of the Advent's
midnight mass. Traditional is a concert on the

steps of *Number 11* by the square's own music makers, the Beacon Hill Hand Bell Ringers Band, who are later joined by groups of wandering carolers.

Prominent people have always lived here. William Dean Howells, the eminent editor of *The Atlantic Monthly*, owned Number 4 during the 1890's. Louisa May Alcott lived with her father as tenant at Number 10. And Number 20 is pointed out by every guidebook as the setting of Jenny Lind's marriage in 1852 to her accompanist. The house belonged to Samuel Ward, Julia Ward Howe's brother, who represented the bride's London agents. A more recent nuptial affair was the reception for the daughter of a late hotel magnate, which took place al fresco — a gala, though temporary, "embellishment of the grass area." Yet another wedding is recalled which is associated with Number 8. In 1923 this beautiful facade was fitted with a new and very thorough Georgian interior as a gift to his bride by William K. Vanderbilt.

All this is familiar to the Hill-dweller, to whom the square is personified as a neighborhood friend. From evidence of pram at doorstep and exodus of eight o'clock scholar with school bag and hockey stick, there is hope that future generations will share this affection.

If one may rise to the metaphor that Boston wears Beacon Hill as a brooch upon its cityscape — then, indeed, Louisburg Square is the gemstone.

North Slope

O NE CAN SEE from the map that Pinckney Street divides Beacon Hill into fairly equal north and south acreage. One also appreciates, after ascending Pinckney, that it extends along the height of the hill. To the south the land falls more or less gradually to Beacon Street. To the north there is quite a steep pitch down to Cambridge Street. This side of the hill has become known as the North Slope, and as we have observed, developed earlier and independently of the hill's opposite side. It also developed less virtuously. Nearer the waterfront this part of Boston attracted the bawdy houses, to become the city's first "combat zone." With the building-up of the South Slope the Mount Vernon Proprietors, sensitive to social nuances that could affect property values, used Pinckney Street for a wall, opening the long block from Joy to West Cedar northward only at Anderson Street. This North Slope–South Slope attitude lingered on as a concern until after the era of the World Wars. Today the distinction is mostly architectural.

Although the grid of North Slope streets lacks the visual continuity to encourage a random walk, certain houses, courtways, and almost hidden enclaves are typical of a historical period and uniquely charming. But for rare exceptions, the original wooden houses have been replaced, many by rows of tenements built to absorb the rapid population expansion in the last decades of the nineteenth century.

But there is that rare exception, Smith Court. West off Joy below the Myrtle Street corner we step into the early 1800's. The large wooden house at *Number 3* may have been built just before the turn of the last century by Thomas Lancaster and Benjamin Brigham, who, oddly it seems, were bricklayers rather than carpenters. It has weathered the vicissitudes of years and a 1924 renovation. Now it seems the paterfamilias of the cluster of small wooden houses which may be almost its age. Across the lane is a brick structure of an appealingly simple dignity. A stone plaque set in the masonry above the doors states, "A Gift to Cato Gardner first supporter of this building 1806." Built by the African Baptist Church Society, it functioned as both church and school for the Negro population of the neighborhood. Here in 1832 the New England Anti-Slavery Society, led by William Lloyd Garrison, had its beginning. The old structure has been a synagogue until recent years. Now it houses the Afro-American Museum, carefully restored after a recent fire.

Back on Joy Street observe the two large, sturdily built buildings with wide central openings at *Numbers 36–40*. These were built as stables in the middle of the last century to serve the community on a commercial basis — only the mansion house commanded a private stable. The commodious premises housed horses, carriages, and, on the top floor, liverymen. In the Scott Fitzgerald era of the twenties, occupancy responded to the temper of the times, and the stables were period settings for Boston's Bohemia. A group of talented avant-garde quartered here expressed themselves gastronomically as well as theatrically. For a time an enterprise known as the Brick Oven was the haunt of the nonaffluent gourmet. Concurrently a professional repertory group known as the Boston Stage Society was producing contemporary drama of high quality in the converted playhouse at *Number 36*. Boston's first production of Chekhov's *Seagull* was held here. Later, an art colony located in the lofts. Now, the old stables have made effective transition to studios for artists and craftsmen and efficient apartments for the current Hill-dweller.

One block eastward, on the corner of Myrtle and Hancock Streets, is a town house of Back Bay proportions unusual to these slopes. *Number 57 Hancock* merits attention. Glance up the vertical facade to the elaborate mansard roof. The structure was designed in rather a rarefied motif known as Egyptian Revival. This variation of French Second Empire architecture was popular at the instance of the Suez Canal's opening. It may date from 1875, when an agreement was made between Charles Roberts and his westerly neighbor concerning detailed use of their party wall for future construction. In any event, the present house replaced a much older one built before 1816.

While on this flat end of Myrtle Street, the antiquarian may wish to visualize a long, wooden, shedlike shelter of the type that occupied this part of the hill before 1800. Here is the site of the initial American industry, rope making. Boston first produced rope in the 1630's. By the nineteenth century "ropewalks" were a familiar sight and smell on the outskirts of the town. The entwining of hemp was a lengthy process, and the ropewalk building would extend as much as a thousand feet to accommodate it. Within, the ropemaker would walk backward, playing out the fiber from a bundle wrapped about his waist, twisting it into yarn at the same time. Often hot pitch was applied as a preservative, and a ropewalk was considered an odoriferous fire hazard. This was not the aspect romanticized by Longfellow who, in "The Ropewalker," envisions "two fair maidens in a swing," "a schoolboy with his kite," "ships rejoicing in the breeze."

This part of the hill has had a multiused past. After the ropewalks gave way to Myrtle Street, the summit, not far from where we are, was dug down for its gravel. By midcentury, Beacon Hill's most original structure stood here. Consider that the entire north appendage of the State House is built in what once was a great reservoir. Backing up to Mt. Vernon Street, which at that time fronted the north portico of the State House, the embankments of the reservoir soared in lofty battered walls laid up of heavy rough-hewn granite blocks. From a perspective up Hancock the shaggy gray structure with its deeply shadowed vaulting had a Piranesian aspect. Contemporary guidebooks described it with a bit of awe. "A short walk on Beacon Hill brings us to an enormous structure of massive granite masonry which, if the stranger knows not its use, will strike him with astonishment. It is not a jail, though it somewhat resembles one; nor is it a warehouse; nor a church. It is the great Beacon Hill Reservoir, into which flows water from Cochituate Lake, the water which supplies the city with the pure element." In the professional opinion of Charles Cummings, architect for the restoration of the State House, "the most striking example of the right use of granite . . . the noblest piece of architecture in the city . . . a perpetual reminder to every thinking architect who passes beneath its walls of that quality in which our architecture, like our national character, is most deficient — the quality of repose." This is in the 1880's! Built to outlast the pyramids, Beacon Hill's most costly building of its time ($324,127 in 1849, compared with the State House cost of $135,000 in 1798) served little less than four decades. About 1888 it was reduced to foundation stone for the State House's yellow brick extremity — known contemporarily as the "fried egg" and sometimes as the "yaller dorg" extension.

Another last-century granite structure that still exists, indeed has made certain contributions to the present advancement of the arts, is the Church of St. John the Evangelist, midway down Bowdoin Street. A veritable "Rock of Ages," this church typifies the quality of steadfastness so esteemed by the Victorians. The simplified Gothic style is appropriate to the heavy undressed stone. Such is Solomon Willard's architecture. Willard was a talented, practical, yet enigmatic man. A most skillful carver of wood and stone, to him are attributed the beautiful wooden columns of the Park Street Church spire, the fine Greek Revival panels on the facade of the Somerset Club, the Egyptian pylon entrance to the Granary Burying Ground. The construction of Bunker Hill Monument is due to his ingenuity. The church on Bowdoin Street was erected in 1831 for the Congregational Society, pastored by the Reverend Lyman Beecher, father of Harriet Beecher Stowe. From 1863, after the Reverend Mr. Beecher's flock dispersed, the Church of the Advent worshipped here until 1883, when that parish moved to Brimmer Street. At that time the Cowley Fathers made it their mission church.

In the 1960's the central doorway was modified to make entering from the sidewalk less precipitous. A vestibule was created, and the renowned artist Gyorgy Kepes designed the colored glass window featuring the eagle, symbolic of the Evangelist. The cross in the arched panel above is by contemporary sculptor Alfred Duca.

Not to be missed in our peripatetic pursuit of the North Slope are the obscure cul-de-sacs of Beacon Hill, four narrow courtways that so spice this continual feast. Off Revere Street from lower to higher hill are Bellingham Place, Sentry

Hill Place, Goodwin Place, and Rollins Place. The north end of each conceals an abrupt change in land grade. These enclaves of simple brick facades were built up in the 1840's and housed

the artisans and tradesmen of the times. The intimate privacy and quaint charm of these street-ends greatly appeal to contemporary houseowners who make up chauvinistic Beacon Hill neighborhoods.

An architectural delight is Rollins Place, which opens from Revere with the suggestion of a Palladian stage set — except that the structures are real. The pristine Greek Revival portico that

closes the court is functional design. The entrance to the two end houses, east and west, is from the porch, and the facade forms a barrier wall to the drop of some twenty feet.

Yet remaining are certain treasures that must be seen. They are on Cambridge Street. The Burgis map of 1728 shows Cambridge Street curved around the northern foot of Beacon Hill to the banks of the estuary. Along the shores were located three ropewalks, a copper works, and a windmill. By the end of the eighteenth century the east end of the street had developed as a fine residential area. Charles Bulfinch was thirty-seven years old and had proved himself as an architect. Asher Benjamin, ten years younger, was ending his apprenticeship. Of this Federal period two buildings remain. The later, built in 1809, is known as the West Church. It is one of the rare buildings that has documentary evidence of the architect Asher Benjamin. A plan and elevation are published in his *American Builder's Companion*, dimensions are given, and the interior is described. "The size of the house is seventy-five feet square; porch twenty by forty-six feet; to contain one hundred and twelve pews on the lower floor." As a meetinghouse it served until the original Congregational parish dissolved in 1882. Thereafter, the premises were long used as the West End branch of the Public Library and housed a collection of Hebraica. Recently, for a short time it was a nursery school. In 1962 the city sold the building to the Methodist Church, which restored the interiors in a fashion faithful to the period.

Just west, across the rise of Lynde Street, is a Bulfinch prize. It is the first mansion house built by Harrison Gray Otis. Now it is owned by the Society for the Preservation of New England Antiquities, which is headquartered here.

In 1795, Harrison Gray Otis was a budding, thirty-year-old congressman — also, perhaps, he was beginning to develop his addiction to real estate. He requested his friend Bulfinch to design a three-story brick house for his increasing family. Bulfinch's drawing is preserved and presents an elevation very much as it is today. There is a marked resemblance to a Philadelphia mansion which had impressed Bulfinch on a visit to that city. In a letter to his parents he describes it with a certain Boston restraint: "the house of Mr. Bingham, which is in a stile which would be esteemed splendid even in the most luxurious parts of Europe . . . in my opinion far too rich for any man in this country." The Bulfinch drawing shows a piano nobile treatment of balconied floor-length windows above which are garlanded panels. As built, the house has the delicacy of proportion and detail, the lunette, and the Palladian motif that show Bulfinch's affinity for the English Georgian. At a later date a semicircular portico was added to shelter the entrance. It was quite beautifully designed, with handsome Corinthian columns, but in recent years was removed for the sake of authenticity. The interior of the house is particularly rich in period detail. Here restoration is a fine art. Furnishing and decor, scholarship and taste make the society's headquarters a foremost house museum of this country.

Here, at the first Harrison Gray Otis house this pursuit ends — architecturally a decade earlier and geographically on the opposite side of the hill from the third Otis house, which we encountered at the beginning. Between is half a century of historic architecture lived in for more than a hundred and seventy-five years. Reduced to space and time and considered relatively, this may well signify that a continuity of life-style is encouraged by the quality of its setting.

Glossary and Appendix

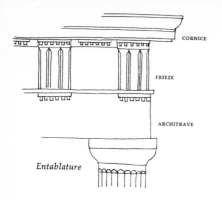

CORNICE

FRIEZE

ARCHITRAVE

Entablature

Oriel

Mansard

Symmetrical Fret

Composite
Capital

Dormer

Palladian Motif

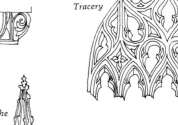

Rustication

Guilloche

Egg and Dart

Tracery

Flemish Bond

Flèche

Acanthus

Portico

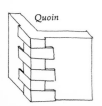

Quoin

Fan Light

Anthemion and Palmette

Glossary

Acanthus	The stylized leaf of Mediterranean foliage, thistle-like, ornamenting Greek architecture — motif expressed in moldings, principally forming the basket capital of the Corinthian column
Adamesque	Relating to a style that recalls Roman classic design, refined and delicate, as practiced by Robert and James Adam, Scottish architects who influenced the development of London and Edinburgh during the Georgian period (1750–1800)
Anthemion	Stylized floral design of Greek motif
Architrave	Horizontal member spanning an opening — the lowest element of the entablature; also the molded framing over door or window. *See* illustration at Entablature.
Baluster	The upright member of a railing or balustrade
Banding	Continuous coursing of masonry
Barrel vault	Continuous arched masonry roof or ceiling
Bond	Brick laid in overlapped coursing to effect rigidity. Types:

> Flemish
> English
> American or running
> Common

Bracket	Supporting member projecting from wall, often used ornamentally in the form of a scroll or volute to carry cornice
Capital	Head or top member of a column
Cheek	Curbing on either side of steps
Corbel	Masonry projection formed by incremental steps, often used decoratively to support cornice

Cornice	The upper member of the classical entablature (*see* Entablature), also the molded projecting horizontal band that tops the wall just below the roof
Dormer	Enclosure with window projecting from a pitched roof
Eclectic	Style that combines designs from various architectural sources
Egg and dart	Ornamental, classical molding
Entablature	Upper section of a classical order composed of horizontal elements (architrave, frieze, cornice)
Fan	Arched transom light resembling an opened fan; often ornamented with delicate tracery
Federal	American version of Georgian architecture, developed during early era of the republic
Fenestration	Window treatment of a building
Flèche	Small spire, usually on roof of church at intersection of nave and transept
French Second Empire	Designating a neo-Roman style current in France during reign of Louis Napoleon (1852–1870)
Fret	Ornamental band made up of repetitive, interlocking forms
Frieze	*See* Entablature.
Georgian	English adaptation of Renaissance style developed during Hanover dynasty (1714–1837)
Greek Revival	Adaptation of Greek motifs in building design of mid–nineteenth century America.
Guilloche	Ornamental braidlike molding of repetitive pattern
Guillotine sash	Window sash opened by sliding vertically in juxtaposition — double- or triple-hung windows
Incised lintel	Head member with engraved or cut-out paneled face
Kenilworth style	Obscure variation of Victorian style replete with romantic, castlelike forms.
Lintel	The horizontal member spanning the opening above a door or window
Lunette	Semicircular recess or opening, usually over door or window

Mansard	Roof in two slopes, with the lower slope almost vertical
Meander	Continuous winding pattern. *See* Fret
Oriel window	Small projecting window corbeled or bracketed
Palladian motif	Treatment of wall opening composed of arch between narrower post-lintel framing — introduced by Andrea Palladio, architect of Italian Renaissance
Palmette	Stylized leaf form used in classical ornament
Parapet	Extension of wall above the lower roofline, often expressed as a low paneled or balustraded horizontal feature
Piano nobile	Exterior definition of upper story by strong expression of fenestration, often by tall windows opening upon balcony
Portico	Brief entrance porch with roof and columns
Post-lintel	Framing members, sills and head, of a rectangular opening
Queen Anne	Phase of late Victorian-Edwardian architecture incorporating various and diverse features — reference implies quality of workmanship
Quoin	Corner member of stone, often used as a prominent feature in the design of a facade
Regency	Phase of the Georgian style (very elaborate) prevalent during the regency of the Prince of Wales — 1811–1820
Reveal	Surface at the side of an opening expressing thickness of wall
Richardsonian	Pertaining to an American style introduced by H. H. Richardson; also known as Romanesque Revival
Rusticated masonry	Large-scaled stonework with individual stones chamfered or outlined in recessed joints to make joints conspicuous
Tracery	Molding within a window, containing glass and forming an ornamental design
Transom	Small window above a door
Victorian	Style embracing a gamut of motifs from neoclassicism to unrestrained romanticism

Appendix: Architects and Housewrights

Only on rare occasions is it possible to identify positively the architect of the Beacon Hill house. Over ninety percent were designed and built by housewrights. On occasion the housewright would find a buyer for the property before the house was built or be approached directly by a property owner with specifications for the design which the housewright carried out. The greater part of the construction, however, was motivated by real estate speculation.

The housewrights copied and improvised from designs in the architectural books of Asher Benjamin and Edward Shaw. With an innate capacity for building, they quickly developed into master builders. The following list is neither complete nor infallible. It has been drawn principally from the gleaning of old property deeds. Where an assumption is made it is followed by (?). Only buildings extant are noted.

Peter Banner	1809 — Park Street Church, Tremont St.
	1824 — 61 Beacon St. (?)
Asher Benjamin	1807 — Charles St. Meeting House, Mt. Vernon St.
	1807 — 54 and 55 Beacon St.
	1809 — Old West Church, Cambridge St.
	1828 — 70 to 75 Beacon St.
	1834 — 9 West Cedar St. (possibly 7 as well) (?)
	1836 — 23 and 25 West Cedar St. (?)
Charles Bulfinch	1795 — State House
	1795 — First Otis House, 141 Cambridge St.
	1802 — 29A Chestnut St.
	1802 — Second Otis House, 85 Mt. Vernon St.
	1803 — 49 Mt. Vernon St. (?)
	1804 — 6 and 8 Chestnut St.(?)
	1804 — Amory-Ticknor House, Park and Beacon Streets
	1804 — 53, 55, 57 Mt. Vernon St.
	1805 — 87 Mt. Vernon St.
	1806 — Third Otis House, 45 Beacon St.
	1806 — 13 Chestnut St.

	1807 — 15 Chestnut St.
	1808 — 17 Chestnut St.
Gridley J. F. Bryant	1846 — 58, 60, 62, 64, 66 Pinckney St.
Cornelius Coolidge	1810 — 74 Mt. Vernon St.
	1820 — 4 and 10 Chestnut St.
	1822 — 12 and 14 Chestnut St.
	1824 — 50 to 60 Chestnut St.
	1824 — 18 and 20 Chestnut St.
	1824 — 7, 9, 11 Chestnut St.
	1825 — 33, 34 Beacon St.
	1826 — West side lower block of West Cedar St.
	1827–1829 — 39 to 45 Chestnut St.
	1828 — 70 to 76 Chestnut St.
	1828 — 36 West Cedar St.
	1828–1829 — Acorn Street
	1829 — 55 Chestnut St.
	1838 — 57 Mt. Vernon St. (entrance)
George Dexter	1850 — 40 and 42 Mt. Vernon St.
Oliver Downing	1834 — 7 and 9 West Cedar St. (designed by Asher Benjamin)
Melzar Dunbar	1831 — 22 West Cedar St.
	1836 — 23 and 25 West Cedar St. (designed by Asher Benjamin)
Loring Dunbar and *Samuel Mitchell*	1834 — 54 Pinckney St.
	1838 — 76 and 78 Pinckney St.
William Ralph Emerson	1884 — 24 Pinckney St.
Jeremiah Gardner	1804 — 47 and 49 Pinckney St. (with Peter Osgood, bricklayer)
	1809 — 23 and 25 Chestnut St.
	1809–1810 — 66 and 68 Mt. Vernon St.
James Garland	1835 — 11 West Cedar St. (?)
John Kutts	1828 — 76 Pinckney St.
Joseph Lincoln and *Hezekiah Stoddard*	1822 — 22 and 24 Chestnut St. (?)
	1822 — 12 and 14 Chestnut St. (designed by Coolidge)
	1823 — 18 and 20 Chestnut St. (designed by Coolidge)
	1824 — 62 to 68 Chestnut St.
	1830 — 12 and 14 Pinckney St.
Ephraim Marsh	1819 — 56 and 57 Beacon St.
	1822 — 48 Chestnut St. (?)
	1822 — 1 and 3 Chestnut St.
	1824 — 63 and 64 Beacon St.

Alexander Parris	1819 — 42 Beacon St.
	1820 — 39 and 40 Beacon St.
	1824 — Lyman House, Joy St.
	1826 — State House gate, Beacon St.
	1826 — Quincy Market, between North and South Market Streets
Edward Shaw	1837 — 59 Mt. Vernon St.
Jesse Shaw	1823 — 28 Chestnut St.
	1824 — 59 and 61 Chestnut St. (?) (housewright, Stoddard)
	1826 — 112 and 116 Mt. Vernon St. (?)
	1835 — 96 and 98 Mt. Vernon St. (?)
	1835 — 22 Louisburg Square
	1842 — 4 and 6 Louisburg Square
Bela Stoddard and *Micah Cutler*	1834 — 27 and 29 West Cedar St. (?)
Solomon Willard	1819 — stonecarving at 42 Beacon St.
	1825 — Bunker Hill Monument
	1826 — State House retaining wall (designed iron fencing), Beacon St.
	1831 — Church of St. John the Evangelist, Bowdoin St.